DARTNELL'S PROFESSIONAL SELLING SERIES

VOLUME 2

CLOSE IT RIGHT, RIGHT NOW!

HOW TO CLOSE MORE SALES FAST

COMPILED BY THE
EDITORS AT DARTNELL

ILLUSTRATIONS: TERRY ALLEN

Dartnell is a publisher serving the world of business with book manuals, newsletters and bulletins, and training materials for executives, managers, supervisors, salespeople, financial officers, personnel executives, and office employees. Dartnell also produces management and sales training videos and audiocassettes and publishes many useful business forms, and many of its materials and films are available in languages other than English. Dartnell, established in 1917, serves the world's business community. For details, catalogs, and product information write:

THE DARTNELL CORPORATION
4660 N Ravenswood Ave
Chicago, IL 60640-4595, U.S.A.
or phone (800) 621-5463 in U.S. and Canada

Dartnell Training Limited
125 High Holborn
London, England
WCLV 6QA
or phone 011-44-071-404-1585

This publication is designed to provide accurate and authoritative information in regard to the subject matter covered. It is sold with the understanding that the publisher is not engaged in rendering legal, accounting, or other professional service. If legal advice or other expert assistance is required, the services of a competent professional person should be sought.

— From a Declaration of Principles jointly adopted by a Committee of the American Bar Association and a Committee of Publishers.

CONTRIBUTORS

Jim Rapp
The Rapp Group Inc.
Alexandria, Virginia

Christopher J. Bachler
Drexel Hill, Pennsylvania

Jenny Hart Danowski
Redmond, Washington

Hal Fahner
Jacksonville Beach, Florida

Dean A. Goettsch
Phillipsburg, New Jersey

John R. Graham
Graham Communications
Quincy, Massachusetts

George Lumsden
Bloomfield Hills, Michigan

Robert Taylor
Sales Counselors
Glenview, Illinois

Tony Alessandra
Alessandra & Associates
La Jolla, California

Theresa Bedal
Barrington, Illinois

Richard Ensman, Jr.
Rochester, New York

Don Farrant
St. Simons Island, Georgia

Jan Goldberg
Glenview, Illinois

Phil Kline
Diamondale, Michigan

Charles C. Schlom
Park Ridge, Illinois

Phillip S. Wexler
Ashtin Learning Systems
Atlanta, Georgia

CONTENTS

Topics include: Two Closes in Every Sale ... Closing — A
Continuing Process ... Checking and Confirming ...
Little Prods That Help ... Natural, Not Obvious ...
Setting the Stage ... Overcoming Buyer Apprehension ...
Customer Commitment ... Commitment to Customer ...
Fear of Closing ... What Does the Customer Think? ...
Quick Tips ... What Would You Do?

Topics include: Alternate or Choice Close ...
Assumptive/Tie-Down Statements ... Trial Close ...
Action Close ... Testimonial Close ... The Weighing
Close ... The Summary or Review Close ... Inducement
Close ... Closing the Invisible Buyer ... Trigger
Phrases ... Keep It Simple ... Closing as a Team
Effort ... Quick Tips ... What Would You Do?

Topics include: Preparation ... Use Staging ... Cover All
the Bases ... Assert Yourself ... Stick to the Basics ...
Practice, Practice, Practice ... Quick Tips ... What Would
You Do?

Topics include: Confirming the Sale ... Seeking
Confirmation ... Buying Signals ... Talking Yourself
Out of the Sale ... Quick Tips ... What Would You Do?

INTRODUCTION

Dear Sales Professional,

Ask professional salespeople to describe to you exactly when they start to close a sale and you're likely to hear.

- When everything is just right
- When I sense that it's time
- When I get buying signals
- I can't explain it. I just know

For these individuals, closing the sale is so automatic, so second nature, that they no longer give it much thought. It just happens.

For others, it's not that simple. They must be more delibrate with the selling process — they have to think about each step, from saying "hello" to getting a signature on the order form. For these salespeople, this book is a gold mine.

All salespeople, new and experienced, will benefit from the combined wisdom of dozens of highly successful salespeople, sales managers, sales trainers, and others who have contributed ideas taken from thier own experiences.

It's impossible to discuss closing the sale without talking about the entire sales presentation and interview. Why? Because closing is so intertwined with all other aspects of making the sale and can come at any time during the sales process. To make the point, consider the salesperson who, upon walking into the customer's office hears, " I knew you were coming today and have decided to purchase a very large quantity of your product. Here's the order!"

The salesperson didn't even have time to say "hello."

That's what you call an early close. While this example is a bit unusual, it does happen and points up the fact that closing should not be, and in fact cannot be, considered in isolation.

Perhaps one reason closing the sale is not well understood is that the buyer, and sometimes the salesperson, cannot identify when the close happened, even immediately after the sale took place. This is because it is so well integrated into the discussion between buyer and seller.

That's what this book is about — showing you how to make your presentation so seamless that the customer at least is not aware of the closing step. This is the mark if the professional salesperson.

Some salespeople believe that if they make a good presentation, answer all questions, and keep smiling, the prospect will say, "I'll take it." Although this occasionally happens, it's not the customer's responsibility to close the sale. Salespeople worth their salt would not allow this to happen.

If you don't believe that closing is all that important, consider that salespeople the world over are judged by the number of sales they close. While other skills are required, the biggest single measure of a salesperson's performance is the volume of profitable sales produced — day in and day out. That requires a lot of successful closes.

In this convenient size, there's no reason you can't keep your copy of *Close It Right, Right Now!* in a handy location at your desk or work area. We hope you'll pick it up frequently throughout the day to uncover a new tip or technique.

No matter how you use it, we hope you have as much fun reading *Close It Right, Right Now!* as we did producing it. Let us know what you think. Fax us in care of "The Professional Selling Series" at (312) 561-4842. We'd love to hear the sales tips that you've developed over the years so we can include them in a future edition!

— The Editors

How to Use the
Professional Selling Series

Volume 1: More Than a Foot in the Door

Topics covered: Tips for time management . . . How to get new accounts . . . Determining who your prospects should be . . . Qualifying prospects, including sizing up a corporation . . . Quick qualifier techniques . . . Making appointments, including getting in to see the "no-sees" . . . Improving telephone skills, including how to get past the gatekeepers . . . Overcoming first call jitters, including proven icebreakers.

Volume 2: Close It Right, Right Now!

Topics covered: Understanding and preparing for the closing process . . . How to read your prospect . . . Overcoming buyer apprehension . . . Fear of closing . . . Little prods that help . . . Types of closes, including action, trial, inducement, and more . . . Steps to the close . . . Customized closes . . . When concessions are called for . . . Closing by phone . . . Managing the hesitation response and the last objection syndrome . . . Handling the bad-day buyer and the indecisive buyer . . . After the close, including add-ons, making the sale stick, and dealing with buyer remorse.

Volume 3: Do You Have Any Objections?

Topics covered: Objections under the microscope . . . Analyzing objections . . . Why you should welcome objections . . . Listening and asking questions . . . Proven objection-managing techniques . . . The price/quality issue . . . Building value into your products and services.

Though the topics covered in each volume are different, you will find that each has:

- *Practical tips* and *suggestions* . . . hands-on techniques practiced by highly successful sales professionals;

- *Stories* and *anecdotes* from sales luminaries to help you plan your approach, and close the sale; and

- Dozens of *Quick Tips* that you can put into action immediately.

CHAPTER 1

UNDERSTANDING THE CLOSING PROCESS

You may be saying to yourself, "Why does this book start with 'understanding the closing process'? I already know what it is — that's when you ask for the order."

You'll discover as you read further, however, that it's a whole lot more. Consider the fact that closing must also occur in the customer's *mind* before you can make the sale. In this sense, the customer is the only person who can really close the sale.

One of the principles often overlooked or downplayed in any discussion of closing is that sa*les are made only when the prospect decides to buy.* There is no magic moment and no surefire phrase that brings the buyer to a decision. To be sure, there are things a salesperson can do to stimulate final decisions, but these are relatively minor to the entire selling process.

Think of yourself as a buyer. What conditions do you have to have settled in your own mind in order to bring you to the point of making a decision to buy? Here are a few thoughts:

- I want to be sure that the product or service is one that will either solve a present problem or prevent a future one. That means the salesperson has to show and tell me what the product will do and how it fits my needs.

- I want to be able to see *value* before I get involved in price. That means the salesperson has to be able to point out features in this particular product that will make it last longer and work better than any other similar product I have seen or am likely to see elsewhere.

- I want to feel that the salesperson understands my needs and is helping me satisfy them. That means benefit selling that is specific and personal in nature.

- I want to make my decision in an atmosphere that has as little pressure as possible. That means I don't want to hear "This is the last one," "the sale ends tomorrow," or "the price goes up next week" unless it is absolutely true. When those expressions are used often, I become very suspicious.

- I want prices quoted clearly and completely. That means I don't want to make a buying decision only to discover that there are preparation, delivery, and installation charges not brought up earlier.

TWO CLOSES IN EVERY SALE

In every sale, there are at least two closes. The first is the buyer's decision that the *product* is right. The second is that the *price* is considered appropriate. To be sure, there are price buyers who announce their economic limits or concerns at the outset of the sale, but a great price on a poor product will seldom close the deal.

Alert salespeople will postpone price talk until there is clear evidence of buyer satisfaction with the product or service. If, as often happens, negotiations are necessary to close the sale, those negotiations are centered on a single product or service. And when *value* has been established in the buyer's mind, he or she may be more yielding on price matters.

Swinging from product to price talk throughout the sales encounter is a classic mistake made by many salespeople.

CLOSING — A CONTINUING PROCESS

Contrary to the popular belief that closing is an "end-game," or a final manipulation that sparks agreement, closing is a constant and continuing activity. I warm to the salesperson who shows interest in me. That helps me decide in his or her favor. I am attracted by a sales presentation that gives me clear information. That helps me favor that product. I appreciate learning about how the product fits my needs and benefits me. That helps me exclude other products I may have considered.

In the absence of all those good things, I am not likely to buy, no matter how clever the salesperson is in trying to button up the sale. In fact, I am driven from closing when I perceive too much cleverness in the procedure.

CHECKING AND CONFIRMING

Conversely, I'm pleased when salespeople check and confirm my understanding and my feelings during the sales encounter. Little questions like "Is this the kind of thing you were looking for?" "Will this satisfy your particular need?" or "Can you see how this feature will minimize your operating costs?" are helpful to both the salesperson and me.

Checking and confirming questions — asked in a friendly tone — underscore the salesperson's interest in me. They also direct my attention to value and needs satisfaction. Best of all, they get me saying "yes." Can you imagine my saying "yes" throughout the process, then saying "no" at the end of it? Not likely.

LITTLE PRODS THAT HELP

It is the buyer who decides, not the salesperson. But some buyers are willing to stand over the decision endlessly if not nudged or prodded a little. The slogan "Ask for the order" still applies. But how?

The easiest nudges I've ever heard came from salespeople who simply said, "OK." Isn't that clever?

Or "How soon will you be needing this?" Just an inquiry, but it helps me move on the decision. Or "You said you needed six, but the unit cost goes down at a dozen. Can you use a dozen?" Let me think — I know a good deal when I see one. Or "This unit will do the job for you. You're making a good choice." I guess I am, and I'm relieved.

NATURAL, NOT OBVIOUS

As a buyer, I want to be nudged in a natural and friendly way rather than be the butt of some obvious psychological move. If the sales encounter has been friendly and conversational — give-and-take — I am not surprised when a little prod is inserted. In fact, I'm ready for it, expect it, and even relish it.

SETTING THE STAGE

Many training sessions put all the emphasis on "the close" and ignore all the events that must precede it.

Asking for the order is really just one of several "steps to the sale" contained within the sales interview. When each of these steps is satisfactorily completed, the final step — the close — can be a casual head nod and a mutual OK.

The steps that precede the close include gaining favorable attention, developing a dialogue, making the proposal, handling objections, and asking for the required action.

Obviously, if you don't get the prospect's attention, your close is headed for disaster. Getting that attention involves a number of factors, including your professional conduct and appearance, your opening remarks, and the smooth handling of your sales tools. Overall, you need to please the prospect as a person as well as present an attractive product.

The next step — the ability to develop and maintain an easy but revealing dialogue — is the mark of a top performer. In almost all sales situations, the dialogue is far more effective than the monologue, or "sales pitch." The dialogue is not idle chatter. Rather, it is a business discussion that the salesperson controls through the use of well-planned questions designed to reveal the prospect's problems and mood. Factors involved include appropriate body language, positive remarks, succinct paraphrasing, good eye contact, and visual aids.

During the proposal, the salesperson outlines the course of action that will correct the problems uncovered in the dialogue. Once again, social interaction plays a vital part. By asking effective questions, the salesperson proceeds point by point to get the buyer's approval. The positive answer to each question is really a miniature close.

The "handling objections" step can occur in almost any part of the sales interview. It doesn't matter when it comes up as long as the salesperson is prepared to handle it. It takes practice to know not only what words to say but also which supporting materials to use and how to project the most favorable body language.

When all these steps are recognized, planned, practiced, and executed, the close can be a very informal end to a pleasant conversation. If the interview has taken some time, it is smart to make a brief summary of the features and benefits and then say something like "Do I need a purchase order number?" or "I'll call this in right now and we will ship today. OK?"

The close, of course, is a very important part of the sales interview, but it is just one part. The steps that precede it are of equal importance. When each is done correctly, the close is easy.

OVERCOMING BUYER APPREHENSION

You may be thinking, "Well, that all sounds wonderful, but with some of my prospects, it takes more than a benefit summary to get the order." This is true, especially on the first call.

The customer wonders: "Will it work? Will I have problems? Is this my best option? Am I making a mistake?"

Since overcoming customer apprehension is a normal part of the selling process, all sales reps should anticipate it and work toward minimizing it.

Many times, sales reps don't understand why a customer may hesitate while making a decision to buy. Chances are that basic decision-making apprehension is the culprit. Some customers are "security buyers" and will shy away from making decisions. They may feel that changing anything might jeopardize a situation or system that, although not perfect, is nevertheless working. They simply don't think a change is worth the risk.

Try the following simple strategies to minimize customer apprehension.

1. **Don't use pressure.** Pressuring a customer into making a decision won't help you overcome apprehension. In fact, it could be just the reason the customer is looking for to extend or delay a product search. Pressure to buy when the customer isn't facing a deadline is a tactic that will usually backfire. If the customer is, in fact, facing a deadline, such as a special price time limit, remind him of this well in advance so that he doesn't feel backed into a corner.

2. **Acknowledge the apprehension.** In many cases, customers would like to be reassured that they're making the right decision. To do this, start by acknowledging the customer's apprehension. Describe a time when you were facing a tough decision and how you finally succeeded in making it. Tell the customer about the apprehension you had. Then, describe the positive outcomes and benefits stemming from the decision. If necessary, ask the customer to think back to other decisions he or she has made and point out how they were successful.

3. **Provide evidence of success.** Whenever you can, show the customer other customers who've purchased your product and are well satisfied with it. Put the customer in direct contact with these people so they can see and hear firsthand about their satisfaction.

If others participated in a trial offer of the product in question, bring them back to discuss how happy they are with the results. This can minimize a lot of apprehension. Also, be sure to review all of the guarantees or warranties that go with the product. These can really help illustrate the "insurances" to the customer that the product will work.

4. **Close with a "closing statement" rather than a "closing question."** One thing you don't want to do with an apprehensive customer is ask a "Will you buy it?" question. Rather, make a closing statement. When you feel it's appropriate to close, simply make a statement of what the next step would be. For example: "Since everything seems to be in order, let me arrange to make delivery next week."

Once you've made the closing statement, remain silent and watch for the customer's reaction. Chances are it will be positive — especially since you've relieved the customer of having to say, "Yes, I'll buy it."

These techniques can help you improve your skill at handling customer apprehension.

CUSTOMER COMMITMENT

As a salesperson, it's your job not only to help the buyer identify a problem but also to help that person commit to solving it.

Face it: Without that commitment, you can't close the sale.

When you *can't* get the prospect to make that commitment to take action on your product as the solution to a problem, it's often because you haven't first gotten a commitment from this person that the problem is worth solving. That step should take place early in the sales process.

Here's what usually happens: Once we understand the buyer's problem ourselves and understand the end result the buyer is trying to get, we often rush to tell all about features of our product that will solve that problem.

But the buyer goes through another step. He or she must first decide whether this problem is important enough to do anything about it, relative to all the other problems he or she might have. That's why we hear: "Well, it sounds good, but I don't think I'm ready to go ahead with it right now." When buyers say that, aren't they saying that, although they've identified a problem, they've also decided it's not important enough to worry about and solve right now?

When you think you understand a problem, you need to help the prospect make the commitment that this problem is worth solving. For example: .

Seller: "I think I understand. Your current system is very slow compared with new technology. What effect does this have on your business?"

Buyer: "We've received a few complaints. The sales force says we're losing business, and the word is getting out that we're slow on completion and miss deadlines. But those may just be excuses. You know how salespeople are."

Seller: "What do you think it means for the future?"

Buyer: "Well, we're hearing enough complaints to be concerned. We can't afford to be labeled 'slow and old-fashioned.' We have to look at upgrading our system."

At the prospect's first admission of dissatisfaction with the slow system, the salesperson could have launched into a presentation of product features. The risk is that the prospect may respond with a remark such as: "Our problem isn't serious."

But, with a couple of patient questions, the salesperson can gain the buyer's commitment that the problem is serious enough to work on solving. Then the next step is easy:

Seller: "Well, I've got a couple of ideas I'd like your opinion on. Here are some approaches that have worked for other companies in similar situations."

Remember: In selling, even if you propose a surefire solution, you don't always get the sale. When buyers begin describing a problem or need, you also need their *commitment* to solve that problem.

COMMITMENT TO CUSTOMER

It should go without saying, but sometimes salespeople need to be reminded that they also must have an ongoing commitment to their customers. Listen to what sales and marketing guru John R. Graham has to say about it:

Your sincere and ongoing commitment to your customers is the only real way to close sales consistently. To show your customers that commitment, there are five things that you need to do:

1. *Learn the customer's agenda.* Far too many salespeople see their job as getting the customer to accept their agenda. No matter what you call it, this is still manipulation — and no customer likes it.

2. *Make the customer's heart go pitter-patter.* The salesperson's job is to generate *enthusiasm*. No matter what a customer tells you to the contrary, more than anything else, people want to feel that what they are involved in is interesting and exciting.

3. *Educate the customer.* The salesperson should be a valuable resource for businesses. It isn't what you sell that's important; rather, it's how you come to be viewed by the customer that counts. The customer who thinks, "I want this sales rep around because this person really has some ideas I can use," will buy because that salesperson is valuable.

4. *Be patient with the customer.* Too many salespeople want to sell *now*. That's understandable because they are pressured by their sales managers to make quota or to move particu-

lar items fast. Don't let anyone kid you. That's not sales. A sales quota is only one benchmark of how effective a sales pro is.

Staying with the customer means taking the time to learn what he or she is thinking and then gauging your approach to fit the customer's schedule. Patience is a virtue. Trying to get the sale in a hurry destroys more future sales opportunities than anything else!

5. *Realize that getting the order is only the beginning.* Some salespeople get the order and forget the customer. A good salesperson understands that once the order is signed, the work is just beginning. It's the follow-through and persistence that pay off.

In effect, once the order is in hand, the salesperson becomes the "customer's agent." That's what *commitment* is all about.

FEAR OF CLOSING

To fully understand the closing process, we must come face-to-face with that old nemesis *fear of closing.*

Why is it that so many salespeople find closing difficult? Even when they have acquired the necessary knowledge and skill, why do they still fail to ask for a buying decision? Even when they know that closing is one of their key responsibilities, why do they continue to end an otherwise successful sales interview without so much as an attempt to close?

Let us assume that all necessary elements of the sale have been properly executed. The call has been properly planned and opened; the salesperson has gained favorable attention from the prospective customer, has discovered his or her major needs and objectives, has presented acceptable solutions to the customer's problems, and has apparently overcome all obstacles.

Remember we are assuming now that the salesperson knows *how* and *when* to close. So why doesn't it happen? Here are some of the reasons:

1. Fear is one of the major reasons — fear of losing a prospect, or fear of being rejected, or fear of being placed in a situation that the salesperson may not be able to handle.

2. Although the salesperson knows when and how to close, in the heat of selling, the opportunity is not recognized.

3. The salesperson lacks the proper understanding about job responsibilities or the nature of the selling process.

If the salesperson has done everything correctly, leading the customer step by step through the selling process, why is it necessary to close at all? Why doesn't the customer take the initiative by asking the salesperson to take the order? *Because it is the salesperson's responsibility to initiate the close, not the customer's.*

When and how to ask for the order is certainly important, but to close or not to close is *basic.* In a nutshell, closing *is* the selling job. That is what you are being paid to do — on every call — with every prospect.

WHAT DOES THE CUSTOMER THINK?

Picture this. You are calling on a potential customer. You did everything right, up to the point of closing. You asked probing questions and listened attentively. You made a very convincing presentation and answered all of the customer's concerns and then left without asking the customer to buy. What thoughts might be going through the customer's mind?

- That salesperson doesn't believe in that product or he would have asked me to buy.

- I guess I convinced her that I really don't need the product, or maybe it's not the best brand for my needs; otherwise, she would have asked me to buy.

- There goes an amateur salesperson, a beginner, or a no-sell artist.

- Perhaps he doesn't think I can afford to buy or that we're not big enough to use his products. I'm a little insulted by his attitude. Does he think I'm too stupid to see the value of his product? Is that why he didn't ask me to buy?

- He used up 30 minutes of my day and didn't ask for an order. What a waste of my valuable time!

Rather than being offended by an order-asking salesperson, most customers expect to be asked and hope their own salespeople are out there doing the same. *They are not surprised when you ask for an order; they are surprised when you don't.* They may even lose respect for you as a professional if you don't ask for the order.

If you suffer from fear of closing, perhaps this explanation of causes will help you overcome the problem. What will help even more is to try out the ideas presented in this book. Remember that the more successful closes you experience, the easier it will be to close successfully.

QUICK TIPS

If you recognize any of these traits in yourself, you may suffer from fear of closing:

- Fear that the customer will say "no"
- Drag out presentation toward end
- Don't easily recognize buying signals
- Desperately hope the customer will intercede and say "yes"
- Reluctant to close by phone
- Voice drops when asking for order
- Ask only for token or trial orders

The more you use the following words, the more closes you'll have, says sales trainer John Fenton:

Increase (for example, production, profit, productivity, on-time delivery)

Improve (for example, customer retention, productivity, employee efficiency, picking rates)

Reduce (for example, downtime, waste, repair costs, accidents, out-of-stocks)

Save (for example, time, money, steps, accounts)

Gain (for example, improved efficiency, increased sales, production, time, money).

All your closing techniques won't do you much good unless you have a thorough understanding of the entire selling process and how closing fits into it.

Salespeople who think they can talk anyone into buying anything with a clever close ignore a basic rule of selling: If you listen carefully — with your eyes and your brain as well as your ears — most prospects will tell you how to close them.

Professional buyers understand the closing process. They hate to be forced to take over the close because the salesperson can't or won't do it.

Summarizing the key points of your presentation, stressing those that the customer was most interested in, will signal the buyer that you're about to close and ask for the order.

WHAT WOULD YOU DO?

My district manager says that I make it too easy for my customers to say "no." She says that I leave them too many "outs" and come across as being too casual when I ask for the order.
How can I overcome this problem?

This is a common problem, especially for new salespeople. It usually comes from earlier experiences of being a customer in a retail store, where there is little or no attempt by the clerk to close the sale. Most young people today, having grown up in a self-service environment, have seldom if ever witnessed a professional salesperson at work.

Perhaps spending several days in the field with an experienced salesperson in your organization, observing how this person handles closes, will help.

Certainly the dozens of ideas presented in this book will help, if you'll just give them a try. Use the word "you" frequently, as you present your products: Instead of saying, "This copier will produce 100 copies per minute," say, "Your new copier will give you 100 copies per minute." This kind of dialogue will let the prospect know that you're there to sell a copier, not just to demonstrate and explain its operation.

In most selling situations, you have many opportunities to close. When you ask for the order early, you put the prospect on notice that you're there to make a sale and you're serious about it.

Good luck.

SUMMARY

If you don't really understand how the closing process works, you're at a great disadvantage. Closing is not so much a process or procedure as it is a state of mind — your mind *and* the customer's mind.

Highly successful salespeople have one trait in common — they *assume* the sale will be closed successfully on every call. The confidence they show is picked up by the customer immediately. The customer understands that this is not simply a friendly get-together, but rather a serious, professional presentation with high expectations on the part of the salesperson.

The salesperson shows commitment and expects the customer to do the same. Everything the salesperson says is drenched with "I expect you to buy" feelings.

The combination of enthusiasm and high expectations on the part of the salesperson has a very positive effect on the customer. In this situation asking for the order becomes a mere formality.

If you suffer from fear of closing, it will soon disappear when you understand the closing process and follow the suggestions noted in this chapter. Read on for more great closing ideas.

CHAPTER 2

TYPES OF CLOSES

To increase your closing percentage, develop a stable of closing techniques and use them as appropriate. Some salespeople have two or three that they use, but more are needed to cover the entire range of sales situations and customers.

In this chapter are eight types of closes. They range from the general to the specific and can easily be tailored to any customer. As you read the descriptions, mark those that you want to try, then take this book with you as a reminder when you make calls.

ALTERNATE OR CHOICE CLOSE

Every salesperson is familiar with the "alternate" close, the choice of two or more ways of buying. For example, "Will this be cash or charge?" or "Would you like to have this delivered, or would you rather pick it up?"

The idea, of course, is to give the customer a choice of two ways to buy so that no matter which way he or she answers your closing questions, the customer has pretty much committed to buying something. You can assume that the close is imminent because you've heard buying signals that indicate the customer is ready to buy, or you have received positive answers to your trial closes.

These procedures are all very effective, of course. But there's another important choice you can give to potential customers that will accomplish the same thing: You can give your prospects the choice of buying what they would like or what you believe would be the best for them. The following example of an alternative close comes from noted sales expert Phil Kline.

I was looking for fishing reels for my two boys, who are in their early teens. I looked at the 30 or 40 different reels on display in the sporting goods department. Then I told the sales clerk which ones I wanted to buy.

He asked permission to ask me a few questions, and I told him that would be OK. "Who is going to be using the reels?" he asked, and "What do you want to accomplish, sir?"

Then he told me that the reels I had chosen were fine for boys my sons' age, but that my sons "would not be that age for long" — and that soon they would be looking for something more sophisticated. This gave him a good reason to show me a couple of spinning reels that were higher priced.

Then he gave me a choice.

"I can give you the two reels that fit your boys right now," he said, "or I can give you some reels that your boys can grow into that will last them for a long time."

What do you think I did? Yes, I bought the more expensive reels. Hey, I was *impressed* with the help the sales clerk gave me. He did his job properly. After all, his job is not to be an order taker but to help customers get the proper equipment for their needs.

No matter what your product, many times customers will tell you exactly what they want when it simply may not be the best thing for them. That's why you need to ask your customers questions. You need to give them a choice.

Sure, you can always get a quick sale by giving customers just what they ask for. Any order taker can do that. But by asking the proper questions and recommending something better suited to the customers' needs, you not only make the immediate sale, but also win customers who will buy again.

ASSUMPTIVE/TIE-DOWN STATEMENTS

You can assume approval with a positive statement that, if said confidently, carries the prospect along with you. Then deliver a short tie-down phrase, such as "All right?" "OK?" "Isn't that right?" "Isn't it?" or "Doesn't it?" You may have thought of tie-downs as usable only with trial closes, perhaps fitting at various times into a presentation for confirmation. Examples include "You like this color, right?" "It suits you, doesn't it?" and "You said the price was within your budget — isn't that right?" But here are some examples of an assumptive statement and a tie-down working in tandem:

- "You can handle the payments on a quarterly basis, OK?"

- "I'm going to use your home address for billing purposes, all right?"

- "We'll be sure your shipment comes next week — isn't that great?"

But these statements don't have to be "one-liners." They can be complete closing statements:

- "You're wise to make that investment *now*, while chemical stocks are low. But there's plenty of chance for profit if the big merger takes place. Am I right?"

- "I'm going to book you for two first-class tickets to Antwerp, and I'm setting you up with Trans-Belgium Auto Rentals. Sound OK to you?"

- "I think you'll be happiest with this combination of tile and lower-wall molding. It will be ready for delivery this Saturday. Are we all set?"

A common master word in the assumptive close is "when." If your prospect wants your product, there is a time when he or she wants it. By centering on the question of time, you require the customer to make a decision to buy without his or her being aware of any forcing.

There are other ways to use the assumptive close, of course: "From what you have told me, you will want the special imprint. May I use this phone to see how soon we can get it?" If the prospect says you can use the phone, she, in effect, says that she will buy the product. The principle of this close is to assume that the prospect will buy and to wrap up the minor details.

Fear prevents many salespeople from using this highly successful technique. Fear that the customer will say, "Hold everything! I didn't say I was going to buy." But what if he does? You then treat it as a trial close, find out what is stopping the prospect, and go on with the sale. If he doesn't object to the assumption, the sale is closed. What can you lose?

TRIAL CLOSE

Most salespeople would define a trial close as a question or statement aimed at testing the situation or "taking the customer's temperature." Of course, we should be asking test questions throughout the sales interview, questions like:

- "Fast and easy, isn't it?"

- "Is ease of maintenance an important consideration?"

- "What do you think, Ms. Brown? Which size do you feel would be most suitable for this application?"

One of the best examples of a trial close may be the "if" or "suppose" questions. For example: "If you were to standardize this unit in every department, how many would you require?"

Good times for a trial close include when you think the prospect might be ready to buy, after making a strong point in your presentation, or after successfully answering an objection.

Don't give up too soon! Use several trial closes until the prospect reacts properly. John Patterson, dean of sales trainers, told his National Cash Register salespeople to try for a close seven times before they turned in a report that a prospect couldn't be sold.

ACTION CLOSE

A study of successful closers will show that they do more than just say something to bring about the close; at the right time they introduce a proposal for action that will close the sale automatically. The technique is closely related to the assumptive close but includes action as well as talk.

The action close is not attempted until the prospect shows signs of being receptive. Perhaps the most common action close consists of writing the order, then showing it to the prospect and asking, "Will you verify this?"

The word "verify" usually works better than "Sign here," or "Will you OK this order?" because it suggests that you want the customer to check the order for accuracy. This type of close is routine when the salesperson prepares a suggested order based on checking inventory or talking with other customer personnel prior to seeing the buyer.

TESTIMONIAL CLOSE

Little used but highly effective, the testimonial close lets a satisfied customer close for you. You've given your presentation and you're ready to ask for the order. You then say something like, "I don't want you to simply take my word for it that our abrasives will save you more than a thousand dollars a year. I would like you to talk with Ralph Martin over at Superior Machine Tools. He's been using our abrasives for three years and swears by them. Shall I call him now and let you talk with him directly?"

Whether the prospect agrees to the call or not, you've really given the prospect only two choices — talk with Ralph Martin or place the order without speaking to him. This technique is especially effective when you're selling large-ticket items or highly complex products.

THE WEIGHING CLOSE

In this close, you ask the customer to compare what will happen if she does nothing versus making the purchase. For example:

- "You say your refrigerator, while still working, is on its last legs and is making strange noises. If you wait until it dies, you run the risk of the food spoiling. What if you're not home for a few days or if the old refrigerator decides to die on Saturday or Sunday and cannot be replaced until Monday or even later? On the other hand, if you purchase today, I will deliver the new unit you like tomorrow and take away the old box. Then you'll have no risk and you'll be able to enjoy your new refrigerator immediately. Shall I write the order now?"

- "Our new perfume line is being introduced next month with a $5 million advertising campaign. All the other department stores in town have already purchased. You can either purchase now and gain full benefits from the advertising or purchase later after your customers start asking for these new fragrances. Which will it be?"

THE SUMMARY OR REVIEW CLOSE

Select the most significant points from your presentation. Hit hard on those that seemed to especially interest the prospect. Say: "We talked about (this) and you agreed you like it. We went over (this) and you said it applied to your daily routine. Then I demonstrated (this) and it was appealing to you. Isn't that right?"

As you get a series of agreements, you have the prospect in a "yes" mood. Now you might conclude: "We agree, then, that this item has major advantages and is priced right for you. I suggest an initial order of (quantity). I can have it delivered in seven days. How does that sound?"

It's a good idea to actually quote, word for word, a positive statement that the prospect made during the interview. For example, "You said you like the idea of offering your customers a wide choice of colors. Well, this line certainly does that and includes bright orange, your favorite!"

Tying the summary and action closes together works very well. Following the example just noted, you might say, "Here's a suggestion for the number of units of each of the seven colors, based on consumer purchases in stores like yours. Take a look and see what you think."

INDUCEMENT CLOSE

A number of closing techniques can be lumped under this heading. They offer an inducement to the prospect to buy right now rather than put it off. One important point about this close, however, is that it should be used only when others fail, when it's a matter of the inducement close or writing off the sale.

Offering an actual premium is a form of inducement, like free service on a machine for a year or a case of soap powder with a washing machine. We all like to get something for nothing.

Insurance against loss is another inducement to the sale. Many individuals aren't particularly interested in making a few extra dollars, but they will fight hard to keep from losing the dollars they have. "Each day you operate without this system, Mr. Jackson, costs you $360. Let's start making the change immediately." "We have one table in stock with the exact finish you want. When that is sold, no more will be available."

There is an infinite number of variations of these closing techniques, and a combination of two or three are commonly used. Certain types of prospects or customers may be better suited to one type of close than another. For example, if a prospect seems dazzled or confused by the complexity of your product or service, you might close by mentioning only one or two features that you believe the prospect will understand.

On a major purchase, such as an automobile, the close should contain a statement indicating that the decision is not only the right one today but also will continue to be right over the life of the car, or until the car is traded in, or the loan is paid off. This might be called a reassurance close.

Salespeople usually have one or two closing techniques that fit their personalities and selling styles and therefore work best for them.

Dorothy Bergman, a pharmaceutical salesperson, uses an emotional appeal when talking to physicians. When closing, she says things like, "Doctor, this new drug is so superior to what you're now prescribing that your patients will feel better immediately once they start using it. They will not only thank you for changing their prescriptions but also tell everyone they know about how you've made their life better. Isn't that what you want?"

Scott Meyers sells temporary help services for a nationally known franchise. When he makes a presentation to an office or personnel manager, he withholds two important benefits until he's ready to close. He calls these his *clinchers*. After describing the types of temporary workers available, prices, and so on, he saves the best for last — two benefits that competitors do not offer.

As he closes and reviews the key points that seemed to be of interest to the prospect, he says, "I want to mention two additional benefits that none of our competitors offer. Either of these benefits, taken alone, would be reason enough to use our services. The first is our absolute guarantee of satisfaction. If you are not completely satisfied with any person we send to you, we will not charge you a penny for their services. Second, we will allow up to one full day at no charge for any of our people who need training at your facility before they can properly handle your work."

If the prospect is on the fence, Meyers says, these clinchers almost always get him or her to say "yes."

So far in this chapter we've talked only about types of closes in the face-to-face interview. What happens if you can't see the main decision maker — the person who must say "yes" before you can write the order? Here are a few ideas.

CLOSING THE INVISIBLE BUYER

In today's marketplace, it is not only increasingly difficult to get in to see key decision makers, it's sometimes impossible. Rather than giving up on these prospects, why not try to reach them through others? Usually you can get in to see an assistant or a technical person, who in turn can take your message to the person who can say "yes."

Here's an example: The chain's reorder person, after you've presented your half-price (for consumers) deal pack, says, "I can take no action. Leave the information and I'll give it to the head buyer." You suspect that this person may not actually pass it on to the buyer, but even if he does, the buyer may give it little attention.

Often, buyers' organizations are set up so that you can see only an interviewer who makes no buying decisions. You explain your services or products to the interviewer, and she sends them on to the appropriate buyer for action. At some chain organizations, a buying committee considers your proposal, along with hundreds of others, each week. Your chances of success are slim.

There are many variations of the problem: The buyer can say no, but she can't say yes; she leads you to believe she is making the decision, but you know she is not.

Most salespeople depend on a face-to-face interview for results. When that is denied them, they feel hurt and either abandon the prospect or refuse to try other devices to close the sale. If you keep in mind that the problem is *closing the sale* and not necessarily *getting an interview*, you are on the way to making the sale.

Remember, your competitors may be having similar problems with the account. With a little effort, you may get most or all of that customer's business.

On the following pages are seven actions you can take when faced with the invisible buyer.

1. Get an advocate inside the customer organization

Find one or more persons — the more influence the better — to carry your cause to the decision maker. With some accounts, this is an obvious person, such as the buyer or assistant. Many times, however, the person is not so apparent, and it requires a little nosing around to find him or her.

One of the best advocates you have is someone who uses or handles your product or the one who would benefit from it if it were ordered, for example, store managers who would save time with your new electronic registers, a chief draftsperson who would save money with your automated equipment, or the warehouse manager whose job would become more predictable as a result of your overnight delivery service.

Personal relationships can also play an important role. Every organization has people who like you and like what you are selling. Not all of them can help you, of course, but if you can find the person who likes you, likes your product, and is also close to the decision maker, you are on your way to closing the sale. Talk with these people. Prepare them to carry your story to the key person. Work out a plan and a timetable. Then put it into effect.

2. Put it in writing

Even if your in-house advocate is your best friend and an articulate messenger, you cannot expect him or her to carry your message effectively without something on paper. You must at least write down the key points of your proposal. Write a cover letter, no more than one page, in which you spell out what you want the decision maker to do. In the last sentence, spell out the *date* and *time* you will call for the order. If possible, schedule a personal visit to the decision maker's office, even though he or she has so far refused to grant you an interview.

Attach your presentation to the cover letter. The first few paragraphs should say *why* you are making the proposal now and describe specifically what it is. The balance should clearly state your case, identifying the benefits that will be derived if the buyer decides to do business with your company.

Test market information, charts, graphs, and financial data may be included as attachments. This will make the presentation easier to read. It may also be helpful to attach one page of questions and answers. These should be concerns that are pertinent to this particular customer and ones that you have encountered in face-to-face selling.

3. Establish that a decision must be made

Regardless of how you get your proposal to the key person, make it clear that you must have a decision by a specific date. This forces action. Even if the answer turns out to be "no," you will probably be given a reason. This information can help you prepare a new proposal.

Some individuals are reluctant to turn you down without a hearing. They prefer to explain to you in person their reasons for not buying. This gets you an interview, which at least is a sign of progress.

4. Establish yourself as an authority

In selling it's always helpful to be seen as knowledgeable about your products and your industry. When the decision maker does not know you and there's little chance that he or she will see you, your credentials become that much more important.

How can you establish yourself under these conditions? For openers, it is essential that the decision maker realize that you understand his or her business and problems So cite specifics when you submit your proposal, whether by letter or through an in-house advocate.

Tell the prospect that you have studied his or her operation, that you have consulted with his or her employees, and that your recommendations are based on these findings. Use names, dates, and places. Refer to your work with similar accounts, too. Do it in a matter-of-fact fashion, not in a boasting way. Understatement is best, particularly when dealing with high-level executives.

5. Work out all the details in advance

In a face-to-face selling situation, you and the buyer can decide such things as shipment dates and billing procedures after the close. Because that is not possible here, you should anticipate these details and assure the buyer that they will be handled properly. If possible, make such decisions yourself and list them on your written presentation. If they must be left to him or her, spell out clearly what the choices are: "Do you want the complete shipment next week, or would you like half of it then and the balance in one month?"

Provide as few choices as possible. In fact, the likelihood of the decision maker's saying "yes" increases if you say, "We will work out the details between us just as soon as the order is placed." The key is to present a package that will elicit a positive response quickly and easily. Once you get a "yes," the details will take care of themselves.

6. Use more than one medium of communication

In addition to a written presentation, try to talk with the decision maker by phone. However, do not attempt to close over the phone unless the prospect has seen your written proposal and has talked with your advocate inside the organization. If you get positive buying signals during a phone discussion, immediately ask for an interview. Try not to accept the order at that time unless you are certain that it is a complete acceptance of your original proposal.

To get attention, try sending your proposal by Federal Express or by courier. One clever woman I know sends her more difficult prospects a tape recorder and a tape with her personal message on it. The attached note says, "I'll stop by next week to get your response to the ideas on the tape." When she picks up the recorder, she usually gets an interview.

7. Follow through and follow up

Chances are there are a number of in-house advocates involved. It's also likely that the sale will be done in stages. It's essential to its success that you get all the actors lined up and that each does his or her bit at the proper time.

You are the director. You are calling the shots, so follow up on everything and everybody. Did the buyer tell your story to Mr. Big when she said she would? Did the samples arrive? Did his secretary make certain your letter was on the top of the stack? Did the slide projector that you left in the conference room work? What was the reaction to your proposal? What should you say to the decision maker when you telephone?

Make a checklist and follow it. Do what you say you will do. Your friends are helping you, so don't let them down. This close could be just the beginning.

TRIGGER PHRASES

You're near the end of the sales process. Most of the issues are resolved, and you sense that your prospect is eager to conclude the sale. A close seems right around the corner.

Yet you sense that a few disagreements might still be thrown on the table. "Trigger phrases" can help you at this stage of the sales process.

They help you focus the prospect's attention on any unresolved issues, negotiate any differences, and then go on to close the sale. Trigger phrases stimulate last-minute negotiations and often begin to motivate the prospect to accept a trial close.

When you're on the verge of completing a sale, use trigger phrases such as the following:

- *"Let's see what we agree on."* This simple statement signals to the prospect that you're trying to sort out any conflicts or discrepancies that might remain between you. It also gives you the freedom to summarize points of agreement.

- *"What do we still have to do?"* Here you're asking the prospect what, in his or her mind, you must do to close the sale. Unresolved or undiscussed objections should be laid on the table at this point.

- *"How can I help you further today?"* With this phrase you're offering guidance and help to your prospect. You're making information, analysis, or guidance available to the prospect in any measure he or she chooses.

- *"Should we meet again, and, if so, what should we cover?"* This question actually pulls you away from your close — but might ultimately strengthen your position a bit. If the sale is near, your question might motivate your prospect to answer in the negative: "No, I'm just about ready to wrap this up."

- *"What do you need to make this deal happen?"* A blunt question, right? But it might work well when you're dealing with a tough prospect oriented to the bottom line. If the prospect answers candidly, you understand exactly where you stand — and what you must offer to close the deal.

- *"When would you like to receive the product?"* By using this traditional trial close technique, you're opening a new line of discussion. Since you probably have some control over delivery terms, you may give yourself some negotiating leverage to wrap things up.

- *"What information do your supervisors need?"* This question works equally well if your prospect must obtain approval or consensus from a colleague or manage-

ment team. You're motivating the prospect to let you
know who else must approve the deal.

- *"How close are we to calling this a deal?"* Without a doubt
this question calls for a direct answer on the part of the
prospect. The trigger phrase motivates the prospect to
reflect on the progress you've made.

Trigger phrases are powerful. They won't guarantee success,
but they can motivate your prospect to go the extra mile in negotiating with you. And that extra mile may well lead to a sale.

KEEP IT SIMPLE

Don't forget how *simple* closing a sale should be. Don't make it
complicated.

One of the ways you can complicate it is by not giving the
prospect the chance to say "yes" after you ask a closing question.
Don't speak first! Give the buyer a chance to buy.

To understand the rationale behind this, consider the *buyer's*
point of view. For her, the last step in the buying process is to take
action on a solution to a problem and to order a product that she
already believes will be helpful in reaching a particular goal.

Because you can't expect the prospect to tell you when she has
reached this point, you need to ask "temperature-taking" and
"trial-closing" questions *throughout* the sales process.

No, you won't hear this from a typical buyer: "Wait a minute.
I'm sold. Don't say another *word* about your product. I'll take it.
And if you were just about to give me a discount, don't bother. I
have no bargaining instinct. Please just take my money and give
me your product!"

Because a sale rarely (if ever) winds up this way, you need to
be alert, at first, for signals that the prospect is seriously considering your product and later, for signals that the prospect has silent-
ly decided in favor of your product.

To prod your prospect, ask such questions as:

- "Now how does this sound?"
- "What do you think of this feature?"
- "Will this produce savings for you?"
- "Do you want this option included on your machine?"

Then, when you're certain that the buyer is viewing your proposition favorably and may even have decided to buy your product, launch a closing question.

If the buyer says: "Well, I *think* that could possibly work in this application."

You should say: "We can deliver September 15 and complete installation September 22. Is that soon enough?"

And then say *nothing* until the buyer responds. If you wait for the buyer to speak, she just might confirm the sale.

If the buyer says: "I've got to start production on a large contract October 1. Will a week be long enough to test the machine?"

You should say: "Yes, easily."

On the other hand, the buyer might respond by raising an objection. You'll have to help the buyer decide in favor of your product with additional facts before you can successfully close the sale.

If the buyer says: "Wait a minute! I said it *might* work. Several features don't make sense."

You should say: "I understand your concern. How can I help?"

And then you need to probe, clarify, restate, handle the objection, and trial close again.

And be silent.

CLOSING AS A TEAM EFFORT

As a rule, salespeople work alone. And, in most cases, that's wise.

But there are times when a team effort is the best way to close a sale. If, for example, you plan to make a presentation before an important group, showing up with another associate or two might elevate your image in that you'll be viewed as being part of a serious team of professionals.

It's best to use a sales team when:

- You're selling a complex product or service
- You need expert assistance in explaining details to the prospect
- You're making presentations for which you will need assistance
- The prospect requests additional input
- You need to deal with several individuals in an organization
- You need to train a new sales associate.

It's best *not* to use a sales team when:

- The prospect is pressed for time
- You're selling something simple
- You can competently close the sale yourself
- The prospect insists on dealing only with you
- There is no pressing need for any kind of assistance.

Team selling can be rather tricky. In some cases, it can slow you down. And there's always the danger that members of the team will contradict one another or somehow be out of sync.

That's why you need to know how to best use your team when you need to and what pitfalls to avoid. Here are some tips:

- *Designate one member of your team as the main spokesperson so your prospect won't feel overwhelmed.* Other team members should speak only when they need to.

- *Plan specific functions for each team member ahead of time.*

- *Choose your partners with care.* When you sell as a team, you're going to be judged as a team. Just as a chain is only as strong as its weakest link, your team is only as effective as your weakest player. Rather than assuming that your strong team members can compensate for the weaknesses of other team members, select only the best help you can find.

- *Limit the size of your team.* Remember the adage "Too many cooks spoil the broth." That's also true in selling. The larger your team, the more confusing matters will be for both you and your prospect. Work with only as many associates as you absolutely need.

- *Plan a strategy.* Your team effort will be much more effective if your group is well coordinated before your first meeting with the prospect. Advance planning not only minimizes or eliminates potential mistakes on everyone's part but also reduces the likelihood that you or your colleagues will talk all at once or compete with each other for attention.

QUICK TIPS

- Keep in mind that you're just one of many people the prospect has seen that day. What you have to say is important to you, but perhaps it's just another "spiel" to the prospect. So give the buyer a break by aiding her memory of your key points by:

  — Summing up your proposition in terms of buyer benefits and positive features

  — Mentioning the shortcomings of the prospect's present method of operation

  — Stating the cost involved

  — Reviewing the return on investment and the profits to be enjoyed

  — Being quiet — and, as a result, "forcing" the prospect to break the silence with either a "yes" or a "no."

- Accelerate the buying decision. People shy away from the final decision. Make it easier for them with a partial commitment: "If I could show you that our product will work more quickly and produce better results, would you consider buying it?"

- Emphasize your guarantee! Don't get so immersed in the product's sales points that you overlook your guarantee. Selling that guarantee is always important — sometimes it's the deciding factor that moves the customer to buy.

- "I'll think it over." Here's one way to handle this pesky objection: Hold back a profit-making selling point — and use it to close the sale.

WHAT WOULD YOU DO?

The sales training course I recently completed emphasized the need to close the sale as early in the interview as possible. I'm not sure I know how to do that. Can you help me on this?

Making the sale is the sum total of the steps you go through from the time you first contact the prospect until he is satisfied with his purchase. All that you do during your selling interview is preparation for the act of closing.

Closing a sale has been likened to buttoning the last button on your coat. As the presentation progresses, you establish the features of your product and the benefits. As the prospect accepts each benefit, it is one more button buttoned. When the last button slips into its buttonhole, the sale is closed. If you have properly established the benefits, all you need to do is write up the order.

Ask a successful salesperson for her one great rule in closing and you will usually hear: "Don't wait too long." More salespeople than we could ever count talk themselves out of a sale by prolonging it until the prospect tires, becomes resentful, or thinks up several more good reasons for not buying.

The early attempt to close may not work, but if it does, think of the time you save for other sales or for rounding up more prospects. Your primary asset as a salesperson is time, and every moment you spend needlessly because you don't close soon enough is a lost moment as far as your income from sales is concerned.

SUMMARY

Salespeople fail to close when they fall short of completing all the steps in the critical path leading up to the close — when, for example, they haven't earned the right to ask for the business or haven't clearly stated the benefits that the customer wants to enjoy. However, when salespeople do cover all the necessary bases, a close becomes the simple consummation of a process that makes sense to both salesperson and prospect.

For this reason, the timing is never right to close early and hard. All that a salesperson can do by following this approach is turn people off.

Never close until your prospect is ready to close. If he or she is not ready to buy, you only increase your chances of getting a negative response.

But how do we know when a prospect is ready? We need to ask trial closing questions to get the prospect's feelings and opinions. For a real estate salesperson, for instance, such questions would include "Is this the style home you had in mind?" "Is this the type of community you envision your children growing up in?" "Would you like the fireplace in your master bedroom, or would you prefer extra closet space?"

From the time that you begin the demonstration part of your presentation, you should be asking trial closing questions about everything that you present. The response of the prospect will indicate whether the timing is right to close. This response also gives you the opportunity to ask if anyone else is involved in the decision making.

In this environment, everything that you ask is nonthreatening. These types of questions cause the buyer to talk and, in so doing, express his or her needs and wants. Such questions also show buyers that you care — that you're interested in something that's good for *them* rather than something that's just good for *you*.

Be sure, though, that when the prospect responds to these trial closes, you are always aware of his or her reluctance and fear of making a buying decision. Make supportive remarks, such as, "I understand how you can see it that way. That was Mr. Smith's concern also until . . . ." And then use the proper benefit that applies.

When a prospect responds to trial closing questions, he is telling you the areas that are most important to him. To make the sale, you need to pinpoint those areas, provide powerful benefits, and show how the benefits outweigh the costs. In other words, you need to convince the prospect that the value he or she perceives justifies the price. The minute that you put *just enough* value into your product or service, the prospect will be motivated to buy — willingly.

Clearly, when all is said and done, timing is the key to closing. So patiently cover all of the steps — and *ask*.

CHAPTER 3

STEPS TO THE CLOSE

In the previous chapter, we discuss many types of closes. In this chapter we review the steps necessary to carry them out and ensure a successful sale.

We've mentioned several times that it is necessary to prepare the customer for the close. We now look at ways to accomplish this. Having a good understanding of these steps will make the closing process much easier and much more rewarding.

PREPARATION

You've worked within the customer's decision-making process and sold all the key players. Now it's time to pull all the pieces together to close the sale.

Closing the sale takes a lot of careful preparation. Here, you'll be presenting the specifics regarding how your product will solve the customer's problem. It's here that all your hard work can pay off — provided you've done all your homework.

There are five important steps to take to prepare for the closing meeting:

1. Set up the appointment. The closing meeting itself may take place one-on-one with the decision maker or it may take place with a few people or an entire staff. Does one person approve a purchase or does it have to be brought before a committee? Do key people have to be there to voice their approval? Whatever the customer's process, you'll need to set up an appointment with all the key people.

2. Organize your facts. Undoubtedly, your product had to meet certain specifications as required by the customer (for example, production speed, tolerances, compatibility with other customer systems). To prepare for the closing meeting, gather and organize your supporting documentation (for example, statistics, testimony, test results). By doing this, you will demonstrate that your product meets whatever specifications have been determined. Try to present numerical performance data by using pie, line, or bar graphs. These can be prepared for the closing meeting as transparencies, flip charts, or handouts.

3. Summarize your work. Prepare a short, chronological outline that highlights all the steps and actions you took in your attempt to sell the account. This summary will help you respond to customer questions with a neat synopsis of

exactly what you did, whom you saw, and when you did it. This summary, which can be handed out at the closing meeting, demonstrates that you've taken the time to learn about the customer's decision-making process and that you greatly value his or her business.

4. Prepare the financing. Often, a debate over financing can delay closing the sale. By the time you've reached the point of trying to close the sale, you should have already discussed and agreed to such key details as price, terms, delivery costs, maintenance costs, lease rates, and payment options.

If you've previously gotten agreement on the financing of the purchase, reviewing the agreement should be a formality. If you haven't, you'll need to negotiate with the customer. Be careful not to grant concessions without knowing the limits your sales management will permit. If you don't have the authority to negotiate, then you'll need to bring in someone who does.

The final step in preparing the financing is to have the paperwork (for example, contract, leases) ready. This way, you can conclude the transaction the moment the purchasing agreement is struck.

5. Prepare the delivery. It's important to check within your company regarding product availability, shipping, and time frame for the installation. This is an important portion of the close. When customers purchase something, they usually want to get it into operation as soon as possible. Customers often plan around the delivery and installation of your product. Don't surprise your customer at the last minute — it may be the last time you do so.

By following these five steps, you will not only prepare for the closing meeting, but also demonstrate your thoroughness and professionalism to your customer.

In the process of preparation, you should give some thought to how you'll let prospects know how you and your company operate. This is especially important with first-time buyers. Let's take a look.

USE STAGING

Salespeople forget that prospects — especially prospects who are currently purchasing from a competitor — are wary of doing business with a new supplier because of the "unknown" criteria of doing business. For a buyer, changing or adding a supplier involves not only assuming risk but also changing buying habits.

An effective way to smooth out this process for the buyer is to put into use a concept known as "staging" — the act of "laying it on the line" for the prospect right from the beginning. The aim is to give the prospect a crystal-clear picture of what it would be like to be involved with you and your company.

Think of staging as a pipeline to a sale. By letting a prospect know up front items such as payment terms, minimums, turnaround time, and so on, a salesperson reduces the odds that a sale will fall apart at the last minute over a simple misunderstanding about how your company conducts business.

To prepare yourself for putting staging to work, make a list of what your customers like most about doing business with you and your company. Positive factors commonly include:

- Installment payments or other attractive financial terms
- A policy of informing customers immediately of complications involved in a job so that they are never faced with unexpected charges or missed deadlines
- A policy of submitting confirmations to customers before delivery or the execution of an order
- A policy of delivering and reviewing all agreements in person to ensure accuracy in the execution of an order

- Verbal quotes available the same day and written quotes within 24 hours.

- Easy accessibility to you via pager, car phone, or personal assistant.

When the timing is right and a prospect clearly understands the basics of what you and your company provide, say something like "when a company does business with us . . . ," and then emphasize the positive and/or unique ways your company does business.

Every such "staging statement" you make moves the prospect closer to closing by increasing his or her comfort level with you. When successfully employed, the act of staging will have your prospects starting to close *for* you. Don't be surprised to hear them volunteer such statements as: "You and I will be negotiating the logistics of this deal, but I want you to direct all the detail work involved to my assistant." You'll rarely hear a statement like this unless you've laid it on the line for a prospect!

COVER ALL THE BASES

In today's marketplace, customers are more demanding than ever of their suppliers — and nowhere is this more apparent than when you try to close. Gone are the days when a salesperson needed only a simple buying signal from the customer to know when to close the sale. Today, sales professionals also need to be able to recognize the point at which they've adequately demonstrated their company's track record regarding quality, service, and performance.

Here's a checklist for helping you know when you've got all the bases covered — and can be sure that it's an appropriate time to try to close the account:

1. Have you followed the customer's decision-making process? Just as each customer's needs are different, so are his or her decision-making processes. In some accounts,

there's a formal, structured process that has to be followed to the letter. In others, there is an informal process of getting a number of approvals for your product. Whatever the process, have you gotten the necessary approvals?

2. Have you reached the decision maker? Hand in hand with knowing the customer's decision-making process is getting to the person (or persons) who can actually approve or authorize a purchase. This is not to say that the other people you've worked with are unimportant. As we mentioned in the previous chapter, these people can influence the decision maker — and thus can be valuable allies in helping you sell.

3. Have you met all the customer's "must" criteria? Everyone who purchases a product has certain criteria that a product must meet as a condition of the purchase. A product, for instance, might have to fit within a certain space, pass specific government regulations, or work within the existing manufacturing systems. Products that don't meet "must" criteria are usually eliminated from consideration.

4. Have you prepared for the competition? You need to develop strategies that maximize your competitive strengths and minimize your competitive weaknesses in your customer's eyes.

   At the heart of this process is a thorough understanding of the customer's needs and of how your product satisfies those needs. You have to recognize the fact that when products are compared, your product can do some things that the competition's can't do and vice versa. Do you have a clear and brutally honest picture of such details?

5. Have you prepared your company? What type of delivery does the customer expect? How often does the customer expect to see a service representative? Does the customer

expect a dedicated account representative? Today's customer is more demanding. Is your company prepared to respond to all of your customer's requirements?

One of the worst things that can happen is for you to assume that your company can or will respond to all of your customer's expectations — only to find out that it can't or won't. Once that happens, will the customer cancel the order because of a perception that a promise has been broken? These issues should be checked out before closing to make sure your company can respond to the customer's expectations.

ASSERT YOURSELF

You will increase your opportunities for a successful sale if you:

1. Expect to close. A sales professional who expects to close presents a confident and knowledgeable image. Prospects sense when a salesperson feels doubt about the outcome of the sale, and they may begin to question whether they should purchase the product or service.

2. Ask for the order. While this sounds simple, it is often the only thing omitted in the selling process. Asking for the order demonstrates your confidence in the product as well as in knowing how to solve your prospect's needs.

3. Don't act wishy-washy. If you want to close, you must be convincing about your product or service. Without enthusiasm and extensive product knowledge, you are doomed to failure. If you seem wish-washy about your own product, how can you expect anyone else to want to purchase it?

4. Don't accept "no" for an answer. It is important to remember that many sales are made after the prospect has said "no." Don't give up when your prospect says, "No, thank

you." Instead, redouble your efforts. You may still be able to turn that objection into a sale.

5. Close with confidence. While it is important to thank your customers for purchasing your products or services, don't overdo it! In the professional selling process, both sides benefit. You make a sale, and the prospect becomes the owner of your outstanding product or service. Close with the confidence of a professional who is proud to share exceptional products and services.

6. Don't rush it. Prospects don't like to be rushed when making a purchase. Give yourself adequate time to explain the benefits of the products or services you are representing, and remember to leave time for customer questions. Rushing sales may increase your number of prospects, but this will not necessarily translate into more customers.

7. Always save one strong point for a final push at the end of the sale. It is important to end your presentation on a strong note. If your prospect is unconvinced at the beginning of your presentation, make certain that he or she won't be able to say "no" after your final point.

8. Get the order and then move on. After you have completed the sale, thank the buyer, ask if there are any last-minute questions, and then move on. Stay only if you have a genuine reason to (for example, networking, answering a question, adding an additional item or service to the order). If you hang around too long after the order is complete, it will appear as if you don't value either your time or the customer's and you don't have important matters to take care of, such as closing other sales. And that, of course, is a false impression!

STICK TO THE BASICS

There are dozens of tips, techniques, and tactics for closing any sale. Some are based on common sense; while others fall more into the category of gimmickry.

But whatever hints you choose to follow to close your deals, there are always the basic proven steps that will not fail you in any situation.

The first of these has to do with the simple act of asking for the sale. After the presentation is over and the demonstration has taken place, after all initial meetings are over and every objection and fear dismissed, *it's time to ask for the order.* This cannot be stressed too often. Unfortunately, many salespeople shy away from this obvious but necessary step.

Another basic tip concerns the timing of the close. Asking your prospect for the sale before all the information has been presented and all the objections have been allayed could be viewed as a "rush job" by your prospect — and be poorly received. On the other hand, if you take too long to close, the prospect might feel neglected and seek out another vendor.

Make sure you know that, at the very least, your prospect is interested in your product before you start the close process. Don't approach him or her for the sale if you know there are still lingering questions. If you haven't done your job to create the desire for the product beforehand, you certainly aren't ready to close.

PRACTICE, PRACTICE, PRACTICE

Some salespeople make botching the close a habit. They can get away with it sometimes if they have repeat business, a rich territory, or expensive advertising programs that generate many successful leads. Their customers buy their products not because of their selling prowess but because they have an overwhelming need for the product. Heaven help that salesperson when customer need shrinks or a new competitor enters the market.

To avoid falling into this trap, salespeople need to practice their closing skills. You need to know how to go for the close. Here is a checklist of tips to help you out:

1. Be neat and presentable at all times. If you look sloppy, the buyer will question his judgment in doing business with you.

2. Keep it simple. Don't confuse buyers with too many catalogs and recitations of technical information they won't understand. They won't be able to decide if they need your product or not — and you won't get an order.

3. Avoid canned sales pitches. Prospects want you to ask questions about their problems. They want to know what the product will do for them in their situation, not how it performs in the abstract.

4. Get to the point. Don't waste time in small talk or meaningless chatter; the prospect has other people to see and other things to do.

5. Have your sales literature organized. Fumbling through it to find just the right piece will distract the prospect from you and your product or service.

6. Be quiet and listen. When you are finished with your presentation, listen to the prospect's questions and respond.

7. Control your body language as much as possible. If you act awkward and uncomfortable, you are broadcasting that you are unsure about your product and presentation. No prospect will risk buying from someone that is perceived as second-rate.

8. Once you ask for the order, be quiet. If you continue to talk, the prospect can delay or even avoid answering you.

QUICK TIPS

- **Make the first move and act.** Too often we approach customers, discuss the product or service, and then don't close the sale. Just because customers want the product doesn't mean that they'll pick up a pen and sign a contract. Making the sale requires effort — don't wait for things to just happen. Give them a pen!

- **Be upbeat about your product or service.** Begging for a sale is not only unprofessional, it's also one of the least efficient and least successful ways of closing a sale. Be positive about your product, rather than try to make a customer feel sorry for you.

- **Convey a sincere attitude.** Sincerity is an important sales trait. Potential customers look to you as an expert and rely on you. If you're flattering customers merely to make a quick close, they'll know it and you'll lose out.

- **Always be prepared.** Learn all about your products and company before you begin to interact with customers. Lack of preparedness translates into lost opportunities and sales.

WHAT WOULD YOU DO?

A sales call gets off to a great start: The prospect's needs seem to match up well with your product, and the prospect seems really open to buying. Is it time for a closing question — already?

It might be too soon for that closing question. You may want to ask some "test questions" first. A test question is like a radar signal that tells you if you're "on course" for closing the sale.

By using test questions, you prompt either agreement or disagreement from your prospect on each point you make. You build your sales story block upon block by making sure that each block is based solidly on the prospect's agreement. You help the prospect make the final decision by first making minor decisions along the way.

Without test questions, you can proceed along in a presentation unaware that you're really building on quicksand because you've failed to detect disagreement from the prospect. Then, when you finally get a turndown, you're devastated to discover that you weren't doing so well after all!

Develop a list of common test questions and think about how you might use them before you make each sales presentation. When typical test questions are programmed into your mind, they surface very easily. Here are some examples of test questions:

- "That's what you want, isn't it, Bill?"
- "We can agree on that, can't we?"
- "How does that look to you, Chris?"
- "That's a beautiful design, isn't it?"
- "Do you see how that will save you money, Alex?"

Each test question should be followed by *silence*. This way, you nudge the prospect to break the silence by making a response — either a "yes" or a "no."

SUMMARY

You have undoubtedly noticed that we continue to stress, throughout this book, the absolute necessity to prepare the customer for the close. The customer needs to get the message early on that you're there to do business, not simply to discuss your products or services.

The customer must also understand who you are and how you do business. There should be no surprises when closing time arrives. When you and your company are new to the customer, certain preliminary information needs to be given before you get into the specifics — who you are; history of the company; your billing, shipping, credit and collection policies and procedures, and so on. Don't assume the customer knows this.

It's also a good idea to briefly cover the strong points of your products or services, in a general way, particularly how they stand above the competition.

Always move from the general to the specific. You're wasting your ammunition if you wait until after the close to mention the company's guarantees, return policy, and so forth, especially if they're strong.

Above all, prepare and anticipate. Decide what steps you will take *before* you see the customer. Anticipate questions and objections and be ready with your responses. Think about when it would be best to do your trial closes. Many times you can lay out your entire closing procedure in advance, particularly with buyers you know.

Don't be concerned that many other salespeople don't bother with this level of preparation and planning. They're not in the top five percent of all salespeople who are truly professionals — the ones that consistently outperform the other 95 percent in their companies or industries.

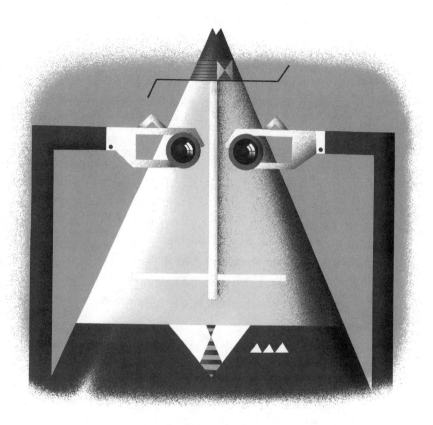

CHAPTER 4

HOW TO TELL WHEN TO CLOSE

The saying "Always be closing" doesn't mean "Apply high pressure."

What it really means is: "Ask for the sale often — but only after you've made it easy for the prospect to buy."

Several retail-oriented wineries in the Santa Ynez Valley of California put this principle into action. On the following page is a look at a typical winery in this region.

Attractive signs out on the public roads invite visitors onto lavishly landscaped grounds with a spectacular view of the mountains beyond the vineyards. Signs in the parking area invite visitors to bring picnics and enjoy a pastoral setting with their wine.

Inside, wood, tile, stone, leaded glass, and fireplaces provide the feeling of a kitchen and great room in a friend's grand home. The tasting room is arranged with samples on a large table.

The servers are well versed in all aspects of wine production and are eager to explain and discuss the variables affecting different qualities in wines and which foods complement which type of wine. Attendants, servers, and tour guides alike are enthusiastic and personable and exude a belief that their winery is the highest-quality producer in the world. They have been thoroughly trained in selling, as well as in industry knowledge.

The typical host and hostess in the testing room say such things as:

- "Yes, that Chardonnay is very mellow. The extra time in the oak cask really shows, doesn't it? The case price allows you to enjoy this for less than the common table wine. Shall I have a case brought to your car, or would you prefer it delivered to your home next week?"

- "That Riesling is our best in several years. We have set aside the entire stock exclusively for delivery to our wine club members. Did I explain the advantages of wine club membership to you? Oh, it's a marvelous idea for wine lovers like yourself. In addition to receiving our best selection each month, a year-round program of tastings, classes, tours, dinner meetings, and cultural events adds a new dimension to your social life and continues to expand your appreciation and knowledge of viticulture. May we include you in our wine club membership?"

- "Oh, you must take the winery tour. It's concise — only 20 minutes — and informative. You'll discover several fascinating secrets of the vintner's art that few know. Shall I sign you up? A group is getting ready to leave in five minutes."

Every visitor is given an opportunity to buy a bottle of wine, a case, a membership for several bottles or a case per month, or a complete package of tours, dinners, tastings, and cases every month. Everyone receives these opportunities not once, but a minimum of six times during a visit. The greeter, the tasting host and hostess, and the tour guide all extend these invitations to buy. Typically, 75 percent of the visitors purchase something, and 20 percent sign up for a monthly membership package.

Think about it. Every person is asked to buy at least six times — and some are asked more than a dozen times. These six to twelve closing attempts take place within just one hour. That's a closing question at least every 10 minutes directed at each new prospect.

And not one of these closing questions makes anyone feel pressured! Everyone enjoys the tour. Everyone wants to return soon. And nearly everybody buys something — happily!

Do you invite each of your prospects to buy six times — in a natural, pleasant way?

"No," you say, "but then my prospects aren't sampling wine in the beauty of the Santa Ynez Valley. They're tough, seasoned buyers who are determined to get the best value for their companies' dollars."

Remember, though, that selling is selling: the *principles* employed by professional salespeople are identical from one industry to another.

CONFIRMING THE SALE

For the professional salesperson, the confirmation is just the beginning of a mutual commitment to an ongoing business relationship. The emphasis is not solely on confirmation of the sale but on the entire sales process. Professional salespeople who sincerely match customers' needs with the products or services they sell can be much more relaxed as they reach the commitment moment. If you've been conscientious all along the way in working with your prospect, the two of you will *naturally* progress into the commitment phase.

Selling is like a marriage. Both parties must make a commitment to each other. When the prospect says "I do" during the closing phase of the sales process, she is making a commitment to implement your solution to her problem. When you say "I do" to your prospect during the assuring phase of the sales process, you are committing to see the solution through to its successful implementation — regardless of what it takes. When you and your prospect make a mutual commitment, you are vowing to have open regular communication with each other and to deal with problems in a friendly professional manner *before* they become too big to resolve.

In collaborative selling, the separation between "selling" and "closing" is barely perceptible. If the sales process up to this point have been done well, the prospect has clearly specified his or her needs and problems and knows how your product or service will specifically solve them. You have had an adequate chance to use verbal and nonverbal feedback to see how the prospect perceives your product or service as *the* solution to his or her goals. In fact, before you enter the commitment phase of the sales process, you and your prospect should have mutually agreed on acceptable solutions to the problems. Therefore, the commitment is not an "if" but a "when." Radical, complicated, or tricky closing techniques are unnecessary.

Therein lie the differences between confirming and closing. It is a qualitative distinction that embodies both attitude and behavior. In the confirming phase, you must be tuned in to your prospect and his reactions. The prospect will determine what you do and when by his or her level of receptivity. If the prospect is ready to commit to a purchase early in the presentation, then you need not finish your presentation. If you continue, you risk overselling or boring her. On the other hand, a prospect may want all the information you have before agreeing to anything. Attempting to gain a confirmation too soon would be pressuring the prospect.

SEEKING CONFIRMATION

When should you try to confirm the sale? There are no cut and dried answers to this. The best approach is to watch your prospect's interest level and buying signals. If, during your presentation, your prospect begins acting and speaking in ways that indicate he or she is ready to place an order, you should stop the presentation and do just that — confirm the sale. You would tie up everything that had been said with a benefit summary and then take the order. A benefit summary is simply a review of all the features and their associated benefits that the prospect responded to favorably during the presentation.

When you are at the end of the presentation process, you and your prospect are ready to proceed to the key phase of the confirmation process — the commitment question.

To do this, ask the prospect an open question with direction, such as "Where do we go from here?" "When do we proceed?" "How would you like to proceed?" or "What's our next step?" These questions are an open, straightforward request, lacking the pushy, tricky, and manipulative characteristics of other closing techniques.

Since your prospect has participated fully in the entire sales process and has had a major hand in collaborating on the solution, you will generally be answered with a time, date, or other relevant reference. If there is some cause for concern, your prospect will generally by this time feel comfortable and trusting enough to speak out. You are, after all, problem solvers working together.

BUYING SIGNALS

All of this points out the importance of being aware of verbal and nonverbal buying signals that your prospect may project. During a presentation, can't you sense whether the prospect is with you or not? Of course! This is because you consciously or unconsciously read your prospect's buying signals. Like traffic lights, these buying signals can be red (negative), yellow (neutral), or green (positive). By the end of the presentation you'll have a good feel for the overall "color" projected by the prospect, and this generally dictates the type of commitment question you would choose.

When the buying signals are definitely red, you simply ask an open question with direction. When you've been getting yellow — or "on the fence" — signals, do a benefit summary and then ask an open question with direction. In some cases — especially with analytical or data-oriented prospects — you might want to substitute the "Ben Franklin Balance Sheet" for the benefit summary. This balance sheet simply consists of two columns of positive features and benefits vs. negative aspects of your product or service.

The only time you should deviate from the open question with direct commitment is when the prospect has been sending definite green buying signals. In these cases, the prospect is basically saying to you — either verbally or nonverbally — "I'm sold." When someone says "I'm sold," what do *you* do? Do you ask, "Do you want to buy?" Of course not! You work out the implementation details such as "How many do you want? When do you want delivery? How are you going to pay for it?" and so on. These questions take the form of assumptive questions or alternative choice questions. It's all right to use these more traditional commitment questions only when you get *green* buying signals from your client. It is not all right to use in all cases, especially when you get *red* signals.

Questions

The questions the prospect asks will tell you a great deal about his or her thoughts. Some typical questions that are buying signals include the following:

1. "Could I try this out one more time?"

2. "What sort of credit terms do you offer?"

3. "How soon can you deliver?"

4. "How can I even think of buying with interest rates so high?"

Questions concerned with terms, delivery, quantities, benefits, and service usually indicate a positive buying attitude. Questions that ask about product features, ease of use, and maintenance are more neutral. Questions that are negative are usually pretty obvious, as in, "This computer was rated tenth by *Consumer Reports*, wasn't it?"

Statements

A prospect may send various positive signals by making statements or comments about the product or service:

1. "That's very interesting"

2. "We could probably afford that"

3. "This is not too expensive"

4. "It's exactly what I need"

5. "That's better than I expected."

Body language

We reveal our thoughts through our posture, facial expressions, and hand and arm movements. If you watch your prospects carefully, you will see many correlations between their body language and their intentions.

Keep these clues in mind:

1. If the prospect is sitting, open arms indicate receptiveness; tightly crossed arms indicate defensiveness.

2. Leaning forward and listening carefully shows interest.

3. Supporting the head with one hand and gazing off into space means you probably have lost your prospect.

4. Increasingly tense postures are not positive indicators. People tend to relax when they've made a decision to buy.

5. Happy, animated facial expressions show you that the prospect is relating well to you and your product.

Having a working relationship, you'll want to do more than monitor your prospect's buying signals. You'll want to know why. This is especially true if the indicators are negative. If you have established trust, you can feel comfortable in asking why the prospect feels as he or she does. If you see that her questions or body language indicate disinterest, you should say something like, "I get the impression that I have lost you. Is there something I can do to get back on track?" or, you can say, "I hear you say *yes*, but I get the impression something else is on your mind. Would you mind sharing it with me?"

Think of your relationship as both of you walking side by side down the same path. If your prospect starts to lag behind, you turn to find out why. If your prospect speeds up, you do the same.

The commitment phase of selling is both a beginning and an end: the beginning of a possible long-term relationship and the end of a single sale with a new customer. Now your work focuses on maintaining that customer and keeping him or her satisfied. Best of all, the commitment process can be a win-win situation without ever sharpening your teeth before going for the client's jugular. If you think of your customers as lasting relationships that need to be cultivated, the jugular attack will be replaced by a clear conscience for you and a sigh of relief from your customer.

TALKING YOURSELF OUT OF THE SALE

When prospects have made a decision to buy your product or service, they want to take action and finish the buying process. The last thing they want to hear is a lot of needless detail. So don't kill a sale by talking it to death. Let your customer *buy!*

Consider the following examples. In each, the prospect is obviously ready to buy — and there's clearly a right way and wrong way to treat the prospect.

- When the prospect asks, "What colors can I get this in?"

Don't say: "This comes in all of the popular colors — teal blue, hunter green, harvest brown, ruby red, and so on"

Do say: "What color would you like?"

- When the buyer asks: "How well does this material hold up in hot, humid conditions?"

Don't say: "This material has been tested under every possible stress situation — cold, hot, warm, dry — and is not affected by the environment."

Do say: "How will you be using the material? Tell me more about your concern with hot, humid conditions."

If a salesperson continues to sell right through such buying signals, he or she can end up losing the sale. Every salesperson knows the importance of recognizing buying signals. Why, then, are there so many salespeople who continue talking and/or fumbling around when they hear them?

Many times the problem is that the salesperson has not adequately practiced what to do next. In a selling situation, there are instances when a salesperson should not have to think about what he or she is going to do next. His or her action or reactions should be strictly automatic.

Imagine a tennis player competing in a key tournament. Many times throughout a game, the player is best served by making a "drop shot," in which the ball carries just barely over the net and then dies. The middle of the game is not the time for the player to have to think: "Hey, this would be a great time for a drop shot!" To be truly effective, the shot must be an *automatic reaction.*

A good tennis player knows that the way to make drop shots come automatically is to work with a coach who sets him up for them. The player practices reacting until he can hit the shot without thinking. Then, in a game, when it is the right situation for a drop shot, the player does it automatically.

When a salesperson gets strong buying signals, he or she should be able to employ a standard close that is an automatic reaction to those buying signals. These closes should be very simple, and the salesperson should practice them in a nonselling situation over and over until they become automatic reactions.

When you get buying signals, you should automatically ask: "Does that price fit within your budget?" or something similar.

If the prospect says "yes," *automatically* hand him or her a form and *automatically* say, "Please put your name here the way you would like to have it appear on our records."

QUICK TIPS

- You can assume that the time has come to close when:

—The prospect has expressed a specific need for your specific product.

—The prospect has asked numerous questions and requested product literature.

—The prospect is eager to see and speak with you.

—You feel that all questions and objections have been answered to the prospect's satisfaction.

—You feel that you have successfully established a business camaraderie with the prospect.

—You have discussed price, quantities, and delivery dates.

- As much as salespeople nearing a close dread hearing the word "no," sales trainer Bill Bishop says that, in the right context, that little word can be music to your ears.

He suggests asking these closing questions, in anticipation of hearing a welcome "no":

—**"Is there any reason** why we can't ship you a test order with the understanding that if you're not happy with it you can send it back and you won't be charged?"

—**"Would you have any problem** with a Thursday delivery?"

—**"Do you have any objection** to our shipping today so you'll have it by next Monday?"

WHAT WOULD YOU DO?

Every so often, I feel customers are about to sign their purchase agreements, and then, after a while, they change their minds. What's going wrong?

The problem may lie in those key words "after a while."

When the customer is ready to sign, there should be no period that you can describe as "after a while." Pure and simple, when the customer is ready to sign, he or she should be handed a pen and a contract.

Your problem is that of many sales reps — they don't know when to stop talking. Reflect well upon the following order busters:

1. **The frosting on the cake.** You're exuberant. One of your toughest customers has all but decided to buy. But, instead of asking for the order, you start filling the customer in on all the goodies about the product that you haven't already mentioned. But why? Why not let him find out about the goodies for himself later on? Sure enough, your goody recital opens up a giant can of worms — and you lose the sale.

2. **Free technical advice.** You have the purchasing agent for a large company all ready to sign a big contract for some extremely expensive industrial equipment. You decide that you want the purchasing agent to make sure she thoroughly understands how the equipment operates. Soon you and she are embroiled in a wildly complex technical discussion. Finally, the purchasing agent tells you that she's wondering whether the equipment might be too complicated for her company's needs. Sorry, end of sale.

3. **The unnecessary testimonial.** Your prospect has pen in hand when you say proudly, "You're in good company. So-and-so is thrilled with the product." The prospect picks up the phone and calls so-and-so for verification and hears about a breakdown of which you're unaware. End of sale.

4. **Too much information.** Customer Davis has reservations about your product's quality. You respond to his doubts expertly — even go a step beyond. You end up confusing him with too much information. You should have quit while you were ahead.

5. **Competitive comparison.** You mention a competing product when you really don't need to. The customer decides she wants to know more about the competitive product. End of sale.

SUMMARY

Salespeople don't always agree on the right time to close. There are several reasons for this. Some salespeople want to be absolutely sure that they've received one or more buying signals from the prospect, so they usually take a bit longer to pop the question. Others will try to close when there's even a slight indication that the prospect might say "yes." They figure there's no harm done in asking, and if the prospect responds negatively, they simply try to find out why the prospect is balking, and address that issue.

Top producers generally agree that it's better to try to close early. First, they save a lot of time, and second, they sometimes avoid a lot of negatives that arise when the prospect has a long time to think about it.

A lot depends on the customer, of course. All else being equal, you're better off to err of the side of the early close. Too many salespeople talk and talk, providing information that the prospect neither needs nor asks for. What the customer thought would be a simple decision has now been made complex by the salesperson who has brought up ten more points to consider!

The salesperson who both watches and listens carefully to the prospect will know *when* to close nine times out of ten. This ability, plus knowing *how* to close, is just about all you need to capture the sale.

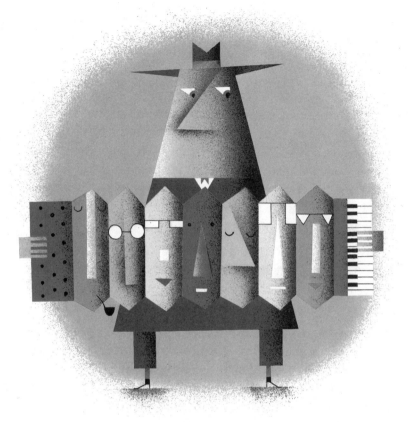

CHAPTER 5

THE CUSTOMIZED CLOSE

With practice, every salesperson can move from simply using a variety of closes to tailoring them to individual prospects and customers. We call this the *customized close*. Salespeople who have developed this technique to a very high level are among the top performers in their companies.

Experts who have seen these salespeople in action agree that they have a natural sensitivity and timing. Perhaps unconsciously they really listen; adjust their close to the customer's personality;

and — most important of all — close only when they have observed and recognized buying signals from the customer.

USE ALL YOUR SENSES

Not surprisingly, most salespeople are talkers, not listeners. Generally the full focus of their attention is on the points they want to put across. While commendable, there are drawbacks: Obvious signals from the buyer can be ignored, overlooked, or misinterpreted. So engrossed are these salespeople in the important things they have to say that they pay little heed to what a customer is saying, or asking, or signaling.

When this happens, the roof is likely to cave in. The order is asked for at precisely the wrong time. Not only have these salespeople failed to listen carefully with their ears, they have not used their eyes or brains to learn how and when to close.

Worse yet, they've failed to size up the kind of personality with which they're dealing. It would be wonderful if every personality could be handled in the same way. But is it really possible to work with the dominant buyer in the same as you might with the customer who is detached or dependent? Not if you want his or her orders.

Dominant personalities are the tough guys — and they're never shy about letting you know it. Look around their offices: awards, trophies, and plaques galore. They *want* you to know they're hot shots. They *demand* deference and respect. They expect to test and control the interview — if you'll let them.

How do you handle such characters? You exhibit a show of strength. Ask for the order. Not once, but again and again. You may never consider them your friends, but you'll win their respect and their business.

At the opposite end of the spectrum are the prospects who lean on you for advice and direction. They're friendly, relaxed, hospitable folks. In dealing with them the salesperson feels immediately welcome in their cluttered offices, usually featuring photos of family and friends.

To close these dependent prospects, you must return their warmth and good cheer. More than that, it is essential to communicate that you genuinely care about them as people and strive to make the buying decision as painless as possible. A good way is to convert big decisions into a series of smaller ones that make it comfortable for the buyer to finally say "yes." Another method is to assume the sale is in the bag. If the prospect reacts passively, your close was right on the button.

Somewhere between the two personality types is the cool, detached customer who seldom exudes much in the way of personal warmth. His or her attitude can be summed up as follows: "Cut out the sweet talk. Just give me the facts and I'll make up my own mind!"

In dealing with this character, you'll be wise to bring plenty of samples and promotional materials. Combined with a logically developed presentation, chances for closing successfully increase proportionally. Be prepared for plenty of penetrating questions, because the detached buyer expects answers in depth — if you want his business.

Don't try to overwhelm the detached prospect with charm. He simply won't buy it. Nor will he put up with high-pressure tactics. Rather, provide solid evidence to support your claims. Demonstrate the logic of buying now. These people respond affirmatively to balance-sheet closes.

The close that casts a spell on one buyer may evaporate when tried on another. This ought to suggest that before any close is attempted, you had better know your man or woman. Read the personality of the person with whom you are dealing, then select the close that best fits that prospect.

READ YOUR PROSPECT

Part of the success of any close rests upon the ability to check for signals correctly. Here are some tips for doing just that:

- Consider timing. How far over are the prospects leaning in your direction? How much more pushing is needed before they finally decide to sign?

- Beware of the shove that can cause the prospect to resist and ruin any chance for making a sale.

- Stop talking! Ask for the order the moment a customer is in agreement with what you've been saying.

- Observe the body language. Give-aways that a customer is coming around to your side include looking at the contract or order, reaching for a pen or pencil, studying samples or sales literature, and doing a bit of figuring on a piece of paper.

While the inexperienced salesperson may find it hard to believe, all buyers *expect* to be closed. The fact is, they're specialists in recognizing the confident sales rep who is making a legitimate proposal. They can also spot the rep who's a bit weak in the knees and unsure of his or her proposition.

If you signal a lack of confidence in what you're selling, how in the world can you expect a buyer to take you seriously? In such situations, problems multiply. Not only will a buyer have no confidence in you, he or she will spend more time looking for flaws and picking your presentation to pieces than listening.

Buyers must first be certain that the product you are selling is acceptable in quality, price, or adequacy. Yet, they want to buy no more quality than is necessary nor less than is acceptable. Blowing quality out of proportion is likely to blow the sale.

Before signing on the dotted line, a buyer must also assure him or herself that the service and delivery you offer is within acceptable limits.

Price never fails to be a huge consideration. All buyers worth their salt usually know instantly whether your price is fair or inflated. They also know that the cost of producing goods goes down as workers become more adept and as other economies come into play. Expect buyers to play hard ball on price when they are confident your firm has lowered costs on a progressive scale.

A closing is not some strange and mysterious art. If anything, it is the *natural* last step in a carefully organized and skillfully presented sales story told clearly and concisely to a customer with a need, the ability to pay, and a desire implanted by you that demands satisfaction.

Yes, customizing your close really pays off.

CORPORATE MAVERICKS

There's one category of buyer that needs a lot of special attention. This personality type can be anywhere, but is more likely to be in the higher echelons of an organization — the maverick.

Corporate mavericks stand apart from their peers. From where they have lunch to their daily work routines, corporate mavericks are perceived as being different — and may be difficult to work with.

Although their unconventional attitudes, values, and goals may not always fit neatly into the corporate mold, these mavericks are still important members of the work team. That means they can be important as prospects themselves or as part of a corporate purchasing committee.

Because of their intelligence and skills, corporate mavericks present many challenges to the sales professional. But meeting the mavericks' challenges can help you upgrade your own sales techniques and open the doors to new sales opportunities.

Here are some tips you can use to solidify your relationship with the maverick:

- *Remember that the maverick needs to be in the driver's seat.* Mavericks often exhibit a frenzied determination to pursue goals and activities they believe are important. You'll often find mavericks working at odd hours, spending their own money on work projects, and smashing through policies and practices to make their visions reality.

- *Listen to the maverick's needs.* When you're working with a maverick, you have to listen — in depth. Your maverick customers will discuss the history of their projects, their current problems, and their short- and long-term objectives. They may go into great detail, even bringing up technical points that you don't fully grasp.

- *Become a true partner.* Because of their independence, corporate mavericks don't have too many real partners in the workplace. They're often delighted to work with someone who accepts them on their own terms. Set out to become their partner and let them know you're there to help.

- *Be a bit of a maverick yourself.* Some sales reps enjoy working with mavericks because the relationship gives them an opportunity to be creative. Build your sales efforts around the interests and work styles of the maverick. For instance, with mavericks who work late at night, you might schedule evening sales meetings at their favorite hangout.

- *Be willing to wait for decisions.* Many mavericks toy with proposals, especially sales proposals, before making a decision. Closing the sale with a maverick can be a lengthy process. Don't push if the maverick isn't ready to close.

- *Offer to help mavericks within their own companies.*
  Mavericks may need help in selling their proposals to
  their peers and management. Let the maverick feel
  comfortable in calling on you for help.

- *Build a permanent sales relationship.* Is the maverick in a
  position to refer you to peers or other companies?
  Persuade mavericks to look on you as a sales consul-
  tant. The personal sales relationship you build with
  the maverick will become an excellent source of high-
  quality referrals — and sales.

TRANSLATION IS IMPORTANT

Imagine a summit meeting between the leaders of two
nations, with neither leader being able to understand the language
of the other. Without translators, the leaders would throw up their
hands in frustration.

Much the same thing often happens when closing. The more
technical your product, the more important your translation of its
features becomes.

It can be argued, of course, that the buyer is operating at the
same level of understanding that you are. But that may or may not
always be true.

Want a good example of the need for translation? Try reading
The Physician's Desk Reference. You won't get far without a degree
in pharmacology or medicine, or a lot of careful training as a
health-care industry sales rep!

Or listen to engineers discuss the products within their spe-
cialties. What you're hearing is a foreign language, indeed!

Of course, at the opposite end of the spectrum are simple
products that literally need no explanation. Some are sold on emotional appeal alone. For example, who has to explain how to pour
milk on cereal, or why to put on a jacket when going out into

chilly weather? But if the cereal has some special nutritional value or the jacket has some unusual insulation characteristic, what then? The point is: Translation depends on the audience and what those people need to know to make the product work for them.

Therefore, in translating your product for your customers, remember to *shift* the benefits in order to meet buyer needs. For instance:

- If your product is to be sold to a manufacturer, emphasize ease of application, durability of material, and other qualities that make the product attractive at the manufacturing level.

- If you're a retailer, shift your story to focus on such consumer appeals as user-friendliness, durability, appearance, and utility.

Remember, too, that your translation should always include an explanation of the *good sense* involved with buying your product. Give your customer a clear and simple rundown of why the benefits work. For instance:

- A car salesperson might discuss acceleration and horsepower with the average retail buyer but stay away from compression ratios and other high-tech talk.

- A computer rep might get extremely technical with experienced systems buyers but stick to basic features with novices.

Here's a good rule of thumb in addressing all kinds of customers: Always keep terminology simple unless the buyer asks for more. Remember that the objective of all translation activity is *understanding*. People buy what they understand and reject what confuses them. The salesperson's function is to translate the difficult into the simple, and thus provide the understanding that leads to acceptance.

When you translate product *function* into product *appeal*, you've added a dimension that leads you to a successful close. When you see yourself as a translator working to build both understanding and desire, you'll see an immediate effect on your closing ratio. Clearly, being a translator *translates* into sales success.

THE SIX-QUESTION APPROACH

When you're trying to switch or replace a customer's current product or service to yours, you may find that asking the following six questions is highly effective. This is the ultimate in customized closes. Ask the prospect:

1. What do you like the most about your current product?

2. Why is that important to you?

3. What do you dislike the most about your current product?

4. Why is that a problem?

5. If you could have something different in your next product, what would that be?

6. Why is that important to you?

Let's look at these questions in action in the case of Bob, who sells carpeting. Bob travels all over the state, does his own installing, and offers a choice of 500 different carpets. And, because he thinks those three facts are important to every prospect, he emphasizes them on each sales call.

We asked Bob to try substituting the six questions for his three favorite facts. Later, he told us what happened.

He asked a prospect what she liked most about her current carpet. She said she liked the fact that, when the carpet was new, its nap stood up straight and looked nice. When asked why that was important to her, she said she liked making her home attractive for parties.

When Bob asked her what she disliked the most about her current carpet, she said she didn't like how the nap went flat after it was cleaned. Bob asked why that was a problem. Because, she said, the carpet didn't look as nice as when it was new. In fact, she said, the carpet looked worse with each cleaning.

When asked what she'd like to be different with her next carpet, she said: "A nap that stands up straight after cleaning."

Bob asked her why that was important to her, and she said that she loved getting compliments about her home and feeling proud of it, not ashamed.

We asked Bob whether he had recited his usual three favorite facts.

"Well, no," he replied. "I didn't have to."

Of course he didn't. That woman didn't care about 500 different carpets, or that Bob traveled all over the state and did his own installations. All she cared about was getting a new carpet with nap that would always stand up straight.

What she wanted to hear — and what she did hear — from Bob was this: "You buy from me, and I'll give you a carpet with nap that will always look good. During your parties, people will always say nice things about your home."

Bob learned that he could greatly increase his chances of making a sale by discovering the dominant buying motive. You can discover it too, with six simple questions.

In addition, you need to provide reassurance that *all* the aspects of your company will be acceptable, not just the product. Now that you've tailored your close through the use of the six questions, you need to find the prospect's biggest concern and resolve it.

Here are some typical concerns and ways to handle them:

- *Price.* When a hang-up over price creates an obstacle and you don't want to make a concession immediately, you can discuss value. Show the genuine worth of your product. For example, say, "This item is not inexpensive, but it *is* economical. You'll get more than a year's usage out of it. Let me show you some of the quality advantages built into it that give it outstanding value."

Price is a widespread concern among sales prospects. But most cases can be resolved by showing your product's advantages. (A tip: Study all your products' features and benefits so it becomes second nature to stress the qualities that overcome price worries.)

* *Durability.* In contrast to price concern, the prospect may be worried about the item's durability. Again, be prepared with evidence of product quality and durability. Show statistics and testimonials that back up your claims.

* *Delivery.* You have given the delivery date, but you can still see that the customer remains apprehensive. At this point, erase any doubt by picking up the phone and calling your shipping manager. Now you have confirmed delivery — and the customer will relax.

* *Service.* Say to the customer, "If anything goes wrong with this, we'll be over to fix it. After all, I'm going to be visiting you regularly to be sure everything is all right." In addition, you may want to show some of your old daily planning sheets that have the service calls clearly indicated.

Other prospect concerns include financing, freight charges, installation, training arrangements, and advertising assistance. If your presentation has been carefully prepared, you should be able to counter each of these worries.

USING CONCESSIONS TO CLOSE

You can customize your close by using concessions. But the concessions need to be *specifically* tailored to the prospect in order to be effective. Many salespeople regard customer concessions warily, but used adeptly, concessions are effective.

Although the usual concession involves price, negotiations are also made on terms, deliveries, freight costs, installation, training agreements, and even tie-in advertising. *How* you concede can be more important that *what* you concede. Here are several tips on making concessions:

- *Give in slowly.* This scenario can occur: Your "too-quick" agreement to a customer's demands triggers caution. "Maybe there's something wrong here," the customer thinks, and then proceeds to demand an even lower price.

  If you must make a concession, do it slowly. In some cases, especially if the prospect presents a number of demands, you would be wise to hesitate.

- *Concede in small increments.* Sometimes a salesperson, eager to complete the sale, will concede not only quickly but in a big way.

  For example, let's say a substantial price adjustment is allowed. Then perhaps more adjustments follow the first. What happens next?

  The prospect, who likes these big chunks of agreement tossed her way, will hold off saying "yes." By hesitating, the prospect hopes the price will keep coming down.

  To avoid this, you have to edge carefully into the arena of concessions with small increments of price reduction or other conditions. Make your concessions in diminishing increments.

- *Give yourself room.* The first conditions you present to the prospect must give you enough room to allow you to negotiate. A price must be quoted at a level that allows it to be reduced. When you negotiate below your borderline price, it's easy to eat up all your profits.

- *Don't be first to concede on a major point.* When negotiating, every salesperson is faced with this question: Who will concede first? If you concede first on a major point, it puts you at a disadvantage. Why? Because the early concession makes you look too eager. However, if there is a minor issue involved, then concede first. The prospect, in turn, is more likely to make a concession on that looming major issue.

- *Respect unrealistic offers.* At times, a prospect may come up with an outrageously low counteroffer. You know it's unrealistic, and you know it would be wrong to concede at this stage. Instead of showing anger, calmly and politely say, "I appreciate your offer, but we're too far apart. I hope you'll take another look at it."

Remember that no one, and certainly not your customer, values things that come too easily. To generate as much buyer satisfaction as possible, you want buyers to believe that they have *earned* the concession in some way. Prospects will then feel better about the sale — and about you, too.

THE IMPORTANCE OF PREPARATION

For most salespeople, most of the time developing a customized close takes thought and preparation before the call. Although you cannot anticipate everything that's going to happen during the sales interview, you most likely know something about the individuals who will be making the buying decisions. Give it some thought. What have they said before? What interests them most — price, quality, style?

Here's a story to make the point.

"I want you to pull out all the stops on this one. That's an important account to open up."

Marilyn McKenzie nodded. She knew only too well how important the Acme account was to her company. She didn't need her sales manager, Joe Fauci, to remind her of that fact. She'd have to make her final presentation to a committee: the president, a vice president, the controller, the purchasing manager, a service technician, and maybe a few others. It was a tall order.

The appointment was for the next day — three days sooner than had been agreed upon. The president had been called out of town at the last minute, and the committee was anxious to make a decision — one way or another.

Marilyn gathered her things together.

"Don't worry, Joe," she told her sales manager. "I'll go over my notes and presentation tonight to make sure I'm ready. And I've got a few angles I haven't told you about. Remember, I've been working on this account for some time."

"I'm counting on you," said Joe. "We're all counting on you. Good luck!"

When Marilyn got home that evening, she opened her briefcase on a card table and began making notes. During the past few weeks, she had met individually with the members of the buying committee. Following each interview, she had written down her observations about the person she'd interviewed. After compiling her notes, the following pattern emerged:

- *President* — Can make ultimate buying decision but relies heavily on the advice of her subordinates.

- *Vice president* — Generally defers to the president; a bit cautious about going out on a limb.

- *Controller* — Very conservative financially, but will readily go along with expenditures that will clearly benefit the company.

- *Purchasing manager* — Not a risk taker. Uncomfortable spending large amounts of the company's money on new programs.

- *Service technician* — A rather quiet, unassuming guy who really knows his stuff.

"Hmmm," thought Marilyn, as she reflected on this last person on her list. She remembered being impressed by the service technician's questions and his knowledge of the plant's operations. He didn't say much, she recalled, but what he did say had made a lot of sense.

"Perhaps," Marilyn mused, "I should concentrate on selling the service technician. He seems to best understand the product and its applications. I might just have an ally there."

Well-rested and well-prepared, Marilyn made a presentation the next morning that was smooth as silk. There was, of course, a lengthy discussion of price, spearheaded by the controller. Once she had answered all the committee's questions, the presentation seemed stalled. Finally, Marilyn turned to the service technician and asked his opinion of the product. He looked up at the other committee members. And then, looking directly at the president, he said quietly, "I think we ought to try it."

Marilyn's secret: thorough preparation and an understanding of the character of each member of the buying committee. By really using her head, she found the extra selling edge that clinched the order.

QUICK TIPS

- In addition to customizing your presentation and your close, you may also want to select a location most conducive to closing the sale, one that fits the prospect, product, and situation. If you have a choice, select a place free of distraction that offers:

    — Good lighting, so that the buyer will have no problem seeing what you want him to see

    — Comfortable seating

    — Adequate desk or table space to display your materials

    — Proper temperature and climate control to ensure the buyer's comfort and wakefulness.

    When planning the setting for a close, make sure that you won't be hampered by environmental factors. Closing an order can be tough enough without starting off with a handicap!

- Close your mouth and the sale. To close more sales, stop talking! Ask for the order the moment your prospect agrees with what you've been saying.

- To truly customize your close, go beyond what the prospect says and consider the motivating factors. For example, a buyer may try to get a lower price, not because she is trying to save money for her employer, but because she wants to be recognized as a shrewd buyer.

WHAT WOULD YOU DO?

A prospect consistently objects when you try to close the sale. You think the prospect is interested but won't buy. How can you measure the prospect's response to your presentation?

Buyers often have a hard time actually saying "yes" to the purchase, even when they want and need your product or service. So, instead of signing on the dotted line, they wait or say, "I'll think about it."

But sometimes, without intending to, buyers signal more interest than they are aware of. Look for some of these responses during your attempts to finalize the sale. These clues may mean the buyer is close to making a decision to buy.

- **Hesitancy.** The prospect may be seeking information in order to make a buying decision.

- **Indecision.** The prospect may need something — a minimum order size or color — to help make up his or her mind.

- **Reasoning out loud.** The prospect may be selling him or herself on the merits of your offer. Don't interrupt.

- **Bargaining.** Negotiation is a sure sign that the prospect wants your product or service but needs to be sure about the price.

When buyers send any of these signals, they may not realize that they've given you a clue about what they're thinking. Take note of this new information and slowly work toward the sale. This is not the time to push too hard for a final decision. Let the sale evolve naturally.

SUMMARY

Customizing the close is not a fine art mastered by only a few. Why then do we witness it so seldom? Because so many otherwise experienced salespeople believe that if they do everything else right, either the close will be automatic or what's said at that crucial point in the interview — how the close is handled — is not a significant factor.

Sometimes that's true. But if the prospect or customer has any lingering doubts that the salesperson has niether detected nor addressed, then the manner in which the close is handled becomes extremely important.

By customizing the close, you add great strength to your presentation and increase your chances of success. You can't rely on a standard close every time, a bit of fine-tuning is usually needed.

Just as fine-tuning benefit statements produces better results, that little extra effort you put into closing pays off as well.

Add customizing and fine-tuning skills to your repertoire and watch your sales soar!

CHAPTER 6

CLOSING BY PHONE

Probably a face-to-face call on your prospect is the optimal selling situation. However, this is not an ideal world. Billions of dollars' worth of goods and services has been sold over the telephone, and more will be sold each year.

Selling by phone will continue to increase because *it costs less* money to get an order by phone than by any other method. No longer is telemarketing thought of as the aluminum siding salesperson on the phone at dinnertime. Telephone sales are now big business in corporate America, earning the respect of hardheaded financial managers everywhere.

No one knows your territory and customers better than you do. Your challenge is to come up with a realistic cost-per-call estimate for every account you visit. Where the profit return appears to be marginal, consider converting that account to a telephone-only account. While your customers may miss the personal contact at first, they will come to appreciate the time you save them by substituting regular phone visits for personal calls.

Selling by phone:

- *Can reduce frequency of face-to-face selling.* Expensive personal contacts can be reduced without reducing your service level or the volume of sales you close.

- *Supports face-to-face selling.* Your customer will appreciate the time-saving benefits of occasionally purchasing from you by phone.

- *Can increase sales.* A well-planned phone call following a personal visit can actually sell more total volume than the personal visit alone.

- *Can make marginal accounts profitable.* Customers too small or too far away for a visit can become profitable telephone accounts.

- *Can find new accounts.* Every seller needs new business to replace those customers who change suppliers, run into financial difficulty, or are swallowed up by larger companies with different suppliers. Therefore, salespeople need a steady stream of new prospects.

YOU ALREADY KNOW HOW

All the closing principles you've been applying in face-to-face calling on your prospects also apply to telephone sales.

Telephone selling can increase the number of customer contacts you make each day, which, considering your prowess as a salesperson, is bound to increase your total sales volume. You need to hone your telephone skills to close the maximum possible number of sales by phone.

Don't assume your customer has time to talk with you. Start off each call by asking: "Is this a good time for you?" If not, ask him or her to name a more convenient time for you to call, and be sure you do it.

If your customer has time to talk, during the first phase of the call, engage him or her in a conversation. Ask questions and listen carefully to the answers, for they will influence your presentation. Be sure to give your customer plenty of opportunities to ask questions. Remember that if your presentation becomes one-sided, with you doing all the talking, you will lose your customer's attention and destroy the bond that the conversation created between you — a bond that must exist if you're going to close that sale.

Without meeting face-to-face, holding your customer's attention can be a formidable challenge. Your only tool is your voice, the words you say, and how you say them. Since the phone cuts off all nonverbal communication, you have to send enthusiastic messages with the tone, speed, and volume of your voice. Speak clearly. Put a smile in your voice. Don't chew gum or smoke. Pronounce the customer's name correctly and use it frequently.

You must use techniques that require customer involvement, maintain interest, and lead you to a positive close.

DON'T FORGET F-A-B

Your selling approach should incorporate features, advantages, and benefits (F-A-B). Of the three, the most important is benefits, which should be emphasized as they address the customer's needs and answer the question "What's in it for me?" When you have your customer's attention, you should ask for agreement on the value of this benefit. For example: "One of the unique features of our vacuum cleaner is that it has a built-in shampoo device. The advantage is that you won't have to buy or rent additional equipment to get this job done. And of course, the benefit is that you will save time and money and have the convenience of cleaning your carpets on a regular basis with no hassle! Wouldn't saving money and having this convenience right in your own home be great?"

Phrased this way, the obvious answer to this question is, of course, "yes." This technique, the tie-down, can be used following your presentation of each benefit of your product. This gets your customer on a "yes" roll: "Yes, that would be great." "Yes, I can see how that would help me." "Yes, that would solve my problem."

Obviously, the plan is to direct this "roll" toward the big "Yes, I'll buy." While not guaranteeing a sale for every call, it sets up a very logical sequence, through dialogue and minor agreements, that is likely to encourage a positive outcome.

Even when the answer to the question "Will you buy?" is "no," this technique serves yet another purpose. It allows you to sincerely and legitimately express surprise and confusion to this negative response since all preceding responses were so positive.

To clarify the customer's thinking at that moment, you might proceed as follows: "Mrs. James, obviously there is something I have not covered that's important to you in making this decision because you've agreed that the features we've discussed so far are just what you've been looking for in a pest control service. May I ask what additional information I could give you at this point?"

In this way, instead of becoming a roadblock, a "no" can become a road sign — showing you the way to continue a dialogue that will dramatically increase your telephone effectiveness. The negative stereotype that surrounds telemarketing is due, in large part, to lack of dialogue. People generally don't enjoy being talked *at* but often enjoy the lively, interesting dialogue that will develop when you talk *with* them about the many benefits that will derive from your product or service.

During your call, be prepared to cite testimonials and references as appropriate.

Keep in mind that selling by telephone carries with it the same ultimate objective as direct selling. Overall, the idea is to gain the buyers' attention, convince them it's in their best interest to listen to you, whet their desire for your product or service, and close the sale.

Keep in mind also that you probably didn't feel totally at ease when you first started selling face-to-face. As you become more comfortable talking to customers over the phone, you'll learn to "read" your customers by careful listening.

IT GETS EASIER WITH PRACTICE

In an attempt to reduce total selling costs, many organizations are requiring their salespeople to obtain more orders by phone, including first-time calls. As much as one day a week is spent on the phone, checking on deliveries, obtaining orders, and so on. Whereas most of these phone calls are to existing accounts, some are to prospects and possibly first-time buyers.

The same closing techniques that work face-to-face work equally well over the phone. Like anything else, it gets easier with practice. You might be surprised at the number of your competitors who call your customers regularly on the phone *and* get their orders at the same time. A famous and highly successful milling company in the Northeast has no outside salespeople. It sells by telephone only to grocery wholesalers and chains across the country. Telemarketing can and is being done successfully.

If you find it difficult to relate to customers over the phone, try these ideas:

- *Imagine you're speaking to a close friend.* For some, this helps create a more relaxed atmosphere during business calls. The point is: Be natural, be yourself.

- *Try smiling during your phone conversation.* No kidding! The listener will actually hear the difference. Over the phone, your voice carries the burden of showing your personality. For better or worse, it always conveys your mood.

- *Speak at a moderate rate.* The rhythm of a conversation is critical. Speaking too quickly may confuse or irritate the listener and get in the way of a response from your customer.

- *Plan ahead to reduce the likelihood of interruptions during your call.* Before you make a call, arrange to have other incoming phone calls held, and try to minimize background noises.

- *Have your calendar or date book nearby.* This way, you won't have to waste time hunting these crucial items down while in the middle of your call.

Because things move along at a faster pace on the phone than in a face-to-face interview, note taking is extremely important. Make notes during and immediately after the call, and be sure to note the following:

1. Date and time of call

2. Purpose of call

3. Outcome/order received

4. Customer's comments and questions

5. What I promised to do

6. What customer promised to do

7. General feeling about conversation

8. Any problems discussed, objections, and so on.

9. Issues to discuss later

10. Date and time of my next call.

INCREASE YOUR PHONE CLOSING RATIO

When your customers understand that you're telephoning to get their order and not to make an appointment or for some other reason, you'll be able to close more sales this way. It may take a while, so don't give up if some customers say, "Let's talk about it the next time I see you." Point out the time-saving advantages for the customer. Explain how you plan to handle the customer's order and stress that you'll always be available if and when the customer needs you.

To be as professional at closing sales on the phone as you are in person, you should be able to answer "yes" to each of these statements:

1. I set up phone appointments in advance.

2. I try to anticipate what the customer will ask, answer, and object to prior to dialing.

3. I keep a record of the best times to reach each customer.

4. I avoid doing something else (such as daydreaming, doodling, or reading) when on the phone.

5. I outline topics to be discussed before picking up the phone.

6. I am kind to anyone who answers the phone because everyone deserves respect.

7. Due to lack of nonverbal cues, I make an effort to use colorful examples and explanations.

8. After identifying myself, I ask whether it is a good time to talk.

9. I leave only result-oriented messages, such as: "Please tell Ms. James that the delivery *can* be made Monday."

10. Once I reach my objective, I immediately end the call — to avoid wasting the customer's time.

QUICK TIPS

You probably suffer from telephone phobia if:

1. You ask others to make calls for you.
2. You don't like to answer the phone.
3. You never call customers unless you have a very specific reason.
4. You lose your confidence when asking for business by phone.
5. You never try to close the sale by phone.
6. You can't think what to say first.
7. You're relieved when the call is finished.

Telephone time savers:

- Act, don't react. Whenever possible, don't answer or make a call when you're unprepared. It's the same as attending a meeting without an agenda.

- Get to the point — fast. Be friendly, but businesslike. Keep chat to a minimum — and cut to the chase.

- Listen for changes in your prospect's language. When you hear "when" instead of "if" or "my" instead of "your," you're getting closer to the sale.

- Tape-record a few phone presentations, then play them back a few times to see how you can improve.

WHAT WOULD YOU DO?

My selling usually consists of face-to-face contact with prospects and customers. By working closely with my customers, I have been able to use body language and facial clues to help me close the sale. The problem is that today much more of my customer contact is over the phone. How can I "read" customers' body language when I'm not there in person?

After having face-to-face contact with customers, it's understandable and makes good sense to use nonverbal behavior to help you close the sale. Posture and facial expressions can be very helpful tools in qualifying a customer and then closing the sale.

Now that you're doing more work on the phone, you'll have to rely on an entirely different set of customer clues. Tone of voice is an excellent way to determine a prospect's moods and needs.

For example, if a prospect speaks in a rushed manner, he or she is probably busy. Your response should be to ask whether there is a more convenient time for you to call back.

If a prospect speaks in broken, fragmented sentences, repeat your reason for calling and make certain that your phone presentation or inquiry is convincing, concise, and clear.

While it's always important to ask prospects if they have any questions, it's even more pivotal when conducting business on the phone. Why? Because valuable customer information may be limited over the phone. Be sure you give your customers plenty of opportunities to ask you questions.

Since the phone cuts off all nonverbal communications, you have to send enthusiastic messages with the tone, speed, and volume of your voice. With practice, you'll be as comfortable selling over the phone as you are at selling face-to-face.

SUMMARY

If the only time you use the phone is when you make appointments or call your office, you're missing out on one of the easiest and best ways to do more business while making your life a whole lot more pleasant.

Don't say, "My customers won't place an order unless I make a personal visit." Chances are quite good that your customers are purchasing many products and services by phone right now and are saving a lot of time for themselves and their suppliers. Consider the thousands of catalog sales made every day. Customers today are experienced in purchasing products and services totally by phone. They like it. Take advantage of it by becoming proficient in making sales presentations and closing sales by telephone.

Making sales by telephone takes a little practice, but you can do it and do it well.

<u>CHAPTER 7</u>

COMMON PROBLEMS IN CLOSING

You almost had that sale. Or at least your prospect led you to *believe* you did. But just before you had a chance to get your project off the ground, the order was canceled.

Why? Just what *was* it that caused the prospect to reconsider?

One explanation is that this was a case of something happening beyond your control. For example, the prospect might have suddenly run into financial difficulties. Or, perhaps, a personal or business crisis erupted at the worst time. Certainly, with any sale, there are countless numbers of unforeseen problems that can pop up at the last minute and ruin the sale for you.

But, you have to admit, all too often when a sales goes sour, it's your fault. But how? Why?

There are many possible reasons, most of which are well within your control:

- *You didn't do your homework.* In other words, you might not have thoroughly researched your prospect before the first meeting. You need to know exactly what each prospect's needs are. You also need to know such crucial facts as whether a prospect is experiencing financial problems.

- *You failed to qualify leads.* If you fail to qualify your leads in advance, you simply don't know what you're dealing with. If you haven't identified the right prospect to begin with, it's not surprising that things go haywire once you're well into your pitch.

- *You talked too much.* There are certain things you need to say, but saying more than you need to can jeopardize the sale. Don't assume that more words are better than too few. Also, let your prospect do most of the talking.

- *You talked yourself out of the sale.* This isn't necessarily the same thing as talking too much. Talking yourself out of a sale refers more to saying the wrong things — which may stem from talking too much, but can also stem from a lack of understanding of your prospect.

- *You talked too much about your company and product, and not enough about your prospect.* Certainly, your prospect needs to learn about you, your company, and your offering. But a prospect needs to learn those things in direct relation to his or her own interests. Therefore, you should focus solely on the prospect and refer to your offering only as it relates specifically to the prospect.

- *You miscommunicated.* Misunderstandings at the outset of the sales process can cause irreparable harm. Once the prospect learns the proper facts, he or she may have a change of heart — and feel some resentment connected with the misunderstanding. This is why it's so important to communicate carefully with your prospect throughout the sales process. Good salespeople leave virtually no margin for error. That's because, unfortunately, some prospects never forgive.

- *You moved too quickly or too slowly.* Move too fast, and you'll lose your prospect. Move too slow, and you'll try your prospect's patience. There's an optimum length for a sales presentation. Find it.

- *You concentrated only on selling, rather than educating, your prospect.* You can be so eager to make the sale that you say what you want to say, rather than what the prospect needs to hear. Forget the vague superlatives; stick to the pertinent facts.

- *You got into a debate with the prospect.* Sometimes a debate is tough to avoid, but remember that you can never win an argument with a potential customer — and there's no value in it.

THE HESITATION RESPONSE

When you have gone through the entire sales process with a prospect only to get a hesitant response, it is frustrating.

You have a right to feel frustrated! After all, you've already made a big investment in the prospect by this point. You've spent hours listening to and questioning the prospect, and trying as hard as you can to understand the prospect's unique situation, problems, needs, and goals.

What's more, you've worked hard to clarify exactly what the prospect wants by listening intently to what the prospect has told you is important to him or her. You've also handled objections throughout the process. In addition, you've been trial closing the entire time you've spent with the prospect.

And *now* the prospect is hesitating. He or she may not go ahead with the purchase! You may lose all of the time and effort you have invested! You may not make your quota this month!

What do you do?

First, try some empathy — putting yourself in other people's shoes. Of course, empathy is easy in the middle of the sale. But when prospects hesitate, it is difficult indeed to think only about solving the prospect's problem and not to think about your own problem: namely, getting the order you've worked for so hard.

But the only way you will solve your own problem is to concentrate only on the prospect's problem. Why would the prospect hesitate?

If you don't know what a prospect is thinking, you should ask. You can say, for instance, "I know this is important to you. You have said you want this very much. What causes you to hesitate?"

Let the prospect tell you. Make the questions open-ended. Don't guess at the reason. The prospect is feeling pressure to take action to solve a problem. The same prospect who was very open with you a few minutes ago discussing her situation may now become secretive and closed to you in order to make the decision. If you ask a closed-ended question, such as "Is it the price?" the prospect believes she has every right to lie to you so she can make her decision privately.

If you're not listening to the prospect — if you're only making statements — the prospect can't take action to solve her problem by buying your product. The prospect can only buy through responding positively to a question.

So you should always ask the prospect another question, such as: "Is there anything we need to consider in addition to what we have already discussed?" or "Which financing method would you prefer to use?"

You may need to reassure the prospect with a quick fact presentation to answer a question, but the basic principle is that a prospect cannot buy in response to a statement you make. The prospect can buy only in response to a question. So, ask the prospect another question!

LAST OBJECTION SYNDROME

Why is it that just when you're an inch away from a sale, the customer always seems to raise an objection? And why is it that this "last objection" always seems to be not only significant, but something the customer had not previously raised as an issue?

Before you panic, recognize that this last objection can be the key to closing the sale.

Realize that customers often object in response to a competitor's offering, or because a superior applies pressure to get a better deal. A last-minute objection can also be a pressure tactic designed to "get the most" from each supplier.

Whatever the reason, your reaction should always be the same: Use the objection itself to help close the sale. Here's how:

1. *Probe the objection.* See what's behind it. If you previously got customer agreement on whatever she is now objecting to, remind the customer of previous meetings, discussions, or correspondence in which the issue was discussed and resolved. Raise the question of what or who is now reopening the issue. Find out why it is being raised now.

2. *Watch for competitors' "incentives."* Oftentimes, competitors add incentives to attract customers. These incentives, however, are often added at the expense of something else. The competitor is often trying to direct the customer away from your proposal by attracting him to something you haven't offered. Review the competitive proposal to find out what the competition is and isn't offering — and inform your customer.

3. *Sell the new players.* If other people in the customer's organization have now become involved in the decision, identify and sell to their needs, too.

4. *Conditionally close the sale.* To handle the last objection, find out specifically what will satisfy the customer. Ask a "what will it take" question, such as: "Since you're not satisfied with the $10.89 price per unit, what price do we have to match to get your next 1,000-unit order?"

   When your customer specifies an acceptable price, indicate that you'll present it to your sales management as the last roadblock to concluding the sale. If the customer agrees to this, you're ready to present this price request to management. If the customer balks, he is objecting to more than just price, and you'll need to probe further. It's a mistake to present this price request to your management without the customer's commitment. If you get the price concession, it will just pave the way for more concession requests.

By following these four guidelines, you'll be in a better position to respond to the dreaded last objection. Above all, remember to keep your cool and manage this final objection in order to move your customer toward closing the sale.

Perhaps one of the reasons you get a "last objection" just before you try to close is that the prospect hasn't really *experienced* your product or service. This is a common problem when you talk about your product but don't really get the prospect *involved* in any way. Let's consider how you might solve the problem.

GET THE PROSPECT INVOLVED

Experience is not only a great teacher, but also a great salesperson. The more you can get prospects to experience your product or service, the closer you'll get to closing.

According to Johann Pestalozzi, the great Swiss educator who pioneered audiovisual aids in the 18th century, the closer you can get a student to reality, the more things mean. Thus, he believed, the best way to educate someone about something is to give that person hands-on experience. Following this in effectiveness would be visuals that simulate hands-on experience, then illustrations, and finally, words.

Measure these thoughts against the most common way salespeople try to educate their prospects about their products. That's right: with words alone! Salespeople start with the step at the very bottom of Pestalozzi's list — namely, they *talk*. They choose the *least* effective way to teach — or to sell!

Now, you wouldn't buy an item of apparel without first trying it on, would you? You wouldn't buy a car without taking a demo drive, would you? Then why do you expect your prospects to buy your product on your say-so alone? You must give your buyers the *experience* they need to give you the *order* you want.

There once was a retail carpet salesperson who was fairly ineffective until he spent a day at the mill watching carpet being made. Back at the store, he was on a whole new kick — enthusiastic about quality and ultrasensitive about decor. He had been moved by *experience*.

And there once was an electronics salesperson who shied away from tough questions until she spent time with a service pro who taught her to check circuits and rewire units. Her hands-on experience went to her head, and her sales improved dramatically. Again, *experience* lit a fire.

Likewise, there once was a *buyer* who was adamant against replacing some antiquated equipment until the sales rep invited him to see a newly completed installation. The accuracy and speed of the newer equipment was so impressive to the buyer that he concluded a deal with the sales rep on the way back to the office. Once again, *experience* caused a big change.

So, the lesson is clear: Lug in the equipment and demonstrate it. Invite the buyer to come to your plant to see the product being made. Cart a buyer over to see a new and effective installation. Get out that video the marketing people put together for you and use it — as well as the charts, the brochures, and anything else that provides more experience than your own sales talk.

Pestalozzi knew a thing or two. He taught folks by letting them experience things. You can sell the same way. Let your prospects see, feel, and operate what you sell. Failing that, give them something that simulates a hands-on experience. Of course, it's OK to talk, too! But remember that words work better in a supporting role than they do all alone.

HANDLING THE "BAD DAY" BUYER

You can feel the tension: You overhear your prospect having some tense words with a subordinate or making sharp demands of a secretary, or she is rifling uneasily through papers. She looks flustered, angry, and disheveled.

Oh, no! The prospect's having a bad day! And this is the day you wanted to *close*!

How do you turn an unpleasant selling scenario into one that produces a "win-win" outcome? The following suggestions should do the trick.

- *Acknowledge the bad day.* Let the prospect know that you understand she is having a rough day. Promise to remain aware of the pressures she is facing.

- *Offer the prospect an "out."* If your prospect is dealing with an emergency, you shouldn't be in the way. Let him cancel the appointment, but try to reschedule it.

- *Learn what's going on.* Ask "Is this time of the year usually bad for you?" Or: "I notice a lot of people having a tough time this morning. Is this time of the week especially tough?" The prospect will undoubtedly appreciate your concern.

- *Let your prospect talk.* She might even want to vent some frustration in your presence. If so, be receptive. You might be just what the doctor ordered.

- *Offer relevant comments about other customers.* "I notice a lot of my customers in this industry having difficulties at this time," you might say. Or: "It seems that all the economic pressure in this industry is creating some very hard times." Comments about other customers will *always* interest your prospect.

- *Follow the prospect's lead.* If your prospect is edgy and trying to move the sales call along, respond in kind. If he seems to lean back and relax as the discussion moves ahead, do the same. Whatever happens, let the prospect take the lead.

- *Use a touch of humor.* Offer a pleasant anecdote about bad days to lighten the atmosphere.

- *Steer your comments toward your prospect's activities.* Perhaps one of the reasons the prospect's having a bad day is because of worries over her effectiveness. Don't come on too heavy, but let her know how your product will help accommodate those concerns. Remember that you are there to help make your prospect's life a little easier. Make this fact known.

- *Close gradually.* Face it: This may not be the time to close. But, if you sense some measure of interest on the part of the prospect, don't add to the day's pressures by pushing to a close. Close the deal on his schedule.

- *Keep everything simple.* If your prospect is having a bad day, anything you can do to simplify the deal will add value to your relationship.

- *Follow up the next day.* Call or send a note that mentions your visit, expresses hope that you'll be working together in the future, and wishes your prospect better days ahead.

QUICK TIPS

- There is nothing as gratifying as the power of new-found confidence when you master the art of closing. With that ability and the great feelings that come with it, nothing can hold you back!

- Keep a special clincher in reserve to throw in if the buyer says "no."

- Temper is never appropriate. You'll be tempted and your good nature will be strained, perhaps often. But if you want to succeed, remember: Control of your temper is a sign of maturity. Both your sales record and your chance of moving up in the organization depend on it.

- You can't fight a paper tiger. If you can't close because the prospect brings up invalid objections, you have to call his or her bluff or ignore these false objections entirely.

- The biggest problems in closing rest directly on the shoulders of the salesperson — closing too late, closing too weakly, or not really closing at all.

WHAT WOULD YOU DO?

I'm a relatively inexperienced sales rep. My biggest problem so far is that whenever I try to close a presentation, I freeze up. Could you give me some pointers?

Closing the sale is the most prevalent problem among new sales reps, but there are some ways to get over the closing jitters. Here are some reassuring things to keep in mind:

- **Selling is about helping buyers make a decision that they want to make.** When you get right down to it, prospects want to buy every bit as much as you want to sell. If you can convince your prospects that you have what they need, they'll jump at the chance to buy from you.

- **Selling is not about someone winning and someone else losing.** If you buy into such a false notion, you are sure to feel rejection each time you fail to close.

- **It's OK to be yourself.** In fact, it's important. Being yourself is really the only way you can project the natural, friendly attitude that can put your prospect at ease. Only when prospects see you as a decision helper and friendly source of information will they be willing to place an order. That's because a sales close is not something that comes at the very end of the presentation. Rather, a close gets in motion from the very beginning of the meeting.

- **You are already a master of an important sales skill: questioning.** You've been an expert at questioning since childhood — so relax and ask away. Questions are not only icebreakers but also essential sales tools. Asking the right questions is the only way to get the feedback you need to give prospects the information *they* need.

- **Closing should be a pleasant experience.** Don't worry about working up to a whiz-bang sales close. You don't need one if you've already received a commitment to your product. Closing is not so much about getting the business as it is about earning the right to ask for the order. When preceded by an honest and thorough interchange of ideas, a closed sale is a matter of satisfaction to both buyer and seller.

- **The prospect is your ally.** So, after you've made your closing statement, be quiet — and listen. You've made your overture, and the rest is up to the prospect. Whether you get the sale or just an opinion, you'll get something useful.

SUMMARY

In this chapter we discuss a number of problems that require your special attention when asking for the order. We're sure you could add to the list, because every salesperson has unique customers and selling situations.

Although you've read in this chapter and throughout the book a multitude of closing problems, situations, and possible solutions, there will be times when you face closing problems that you've never encountered before and have never read about in this or other publications. How should you handle them?

Giving the problem some thought, along with a dose of common sense, will go a long way toward solving these mysteries. If what you're doing isn't working very well, say to yourself, "Next time I'll try another approach." You have to be innovative and flexible — it's as simple as that.

On your next call, try a completely different approach to closing to see what happens. You may be happily surprised!

Chapter 8

After the Close

You've just closed the sale. Great!

But what next? Is that it? A quick handshake, a "thank you," and "good-bye"? Yes and no.

After you close the sale, you are presented with a new relationship with your prospect, as well as new selling opportunities. Your once "hot prospect" is now your newest satisfied customer.

And this, in and of itself, opens the door to a whole new set of commitments to that person. It also opens up a fresh assortment of selling opportunities for you.

But the crucial elements in taking advantage of these new opportunities are timing and presentation. You probably won't want to start asking immediately for quantity increases on the product on which you just closed; but, at some point, you certainly will want to.

Now that your prospect has become a customer, you may also, when the timing is right, present product upgrade opportunities, as well as product maintenance agreements. In addition, you can make complete new lines of products and services available to this new account.

Setting up an appointment to discuss these business concerns is a matter of knowing the right time and place to bring them up. You don't want to appear pushy, but at the same time, you'd like to strike while the iron is hot. After the close is a good time to set up an appointment to discuss further product options or quantity increases. You need to schedule another meeting with the new customer to discuss the possibility of additional sales.

There are a number of potential sales opportunities after a close, such as:

- Quantity discounts
- All-inclusive maintenance, service, or repair contracts
- Additional product supplies
- A new line of products and services.

Be sure to consider all these options with your new customer.

Most important, remember that your prompt treatment of customers after the close will directly affect your future sales opportunities with them.

It's good practice to verify that all product delivery dates have been met and that the equipment has been installed properly. If possible, you may want to be present during installation to see that everything is done properly. Check, too, that the equipment's users have received full training in its use and maintenance.

A few brief phone calls after the close just to ask, "How's everything going?" will quickly convey to your new customer your true concern.

These small after-the-close gestures will help pave the way to future sales opportunities and serve to solidify an outstanding business relationship with your new customer.

MAKING THE SALE STICK

There are times when every salesperson wonders, after a successful close, whether the sale will hold until the product or service is delivered and the customer has paid in full. This is of particular concern when the buyer is extremely hesitant or uncertain during the closing process. Sometimes, especially when a large purchase is made, buyer remorse sets in early and the deal can become unstuck.

There are several things you can do to head off customer flip-flopping. Taking the following steps will go a long way in keeping somewhat shaky sales closed:

1. *Don't allow too much time to elapse between the close and the delivery of your product or service.* A big gap here can be disastrous indeed. When you allow too much time to elapse between the close of your deal and delivery of your product or service, you're giving the customer not only time for second thoughts, but also *cause* for them.

2. *Respond to all of the customer's questions or concerns.* Even after the sale has been made, your customers might have a lot of questions. Don't ignore them! Unanswered questions will always come back to haunt you!

Keep in mind that customers rarely think about all their questions right off the bat. Customers who are resistant to buying from the outset are particularly likely to have questions later. These often might concern issues that the customer believes you overlooked — or deliberately ignored — early on in the sales process. In addition to not being completely satisfied with the product or service he or she has purchased, your customer might also suspect that you are deliberately trying to hide something.

Don't get defensive when such questions arise. Calmly examine each one of them, answer them thoroughly, and do all you can to put your customer at ease. Remember: It's only natural that such questions should crop up in the minds of indecisive people.

3. *Exercise special care.* Don't look past the obvious in dealing with a skittish customer. The fact that this customer was hard to sell might mean that the sale might be difficult to keep closed. All of this adds up to a situation in which you need to work much harder and take much greater care than you might under normal circumstances. It's important to be satisfied yourself that your customer's reservations — even small ones — are eliminated before you can close the sale for keeps.

4. *Learn sufficient details about the customer's business and financial circumstances.* This is an area of major importance because it often accounts for a customer's change of heart. There might be a sudden financial problem. Or the customer's needs may have suddenly changed. Perhaps a competitor has since offered the customer an attractive deal. A number of different factors may adversely influence the outcome of a sale.

Therefore, make sure you thoroughly understand the circumstances surrounding your customer's industry and business. Businesses that undergo dramatic changes can cause problems.

THE ADD-ON CLOSE

The close is a logical and workable point at which to increase the total sales. But how do you add more to the deal? Try these three tips:

- *Suggest a bigger order.* Researchers have found that simply asking for larger orders increases the chance that they will come about. The reason? Apparently, it's easier for people to respond to a specific request than to make a buying decision alone.

  For example, let's say it's your habit to ask prospects at closing time to buy *five* units of an item, because you figure that five will be their limit. Ask them to buy 25, however, and they may end up taking 15 or 20 — and maybe even 25!

  Maybe you're in computer sales, calling on small businesses. You take in a customer's entire operation in a "walk-through," and here and there you see several workstations where your product is obviously needed. On closer investigation, however, you spot other locations where computers would clearly benefit the operation.

  "Based on my observations today, I'm going to suggest an investment in 10 units," you can say, "and show you how it will save you time and money."

- *Offer a choice on a secondary item.* The theory behind this is that it's easier to make a small decision than a big one. You ask for a minor decision that relates in some way to the main issue — and this consequently carries the major decision right along with it!

Let's say the prospect has been looking at furniture but is undecided. You help things along by saying: "Would you like these two matching end tables with your living room suite — or one end table plus the dark oak coffee table?"

When the prospect voices a choice, not only has he bought the smaller items, but the whole living room suite as well.

- *Try the "add-on close."* This close is similar to the "choice close," but different in that the salesperson prescribes an added piece that she knows will attract the prospect. Insurance agents, for example, offer an extra rider, option, or clause with the main policy. Be authoritative about such add-ons. Say: "Here's something else you're going to need" or "Let's look at something that goes right along with it." Remember: When the prospect agrees to the add-on, he or she has agreed to buy the main unit as well.

Put these ideas in motion, and expand the sale with some creative thinking.

DELAYING THE CLOSE

Go for the close? Not always! Sounds strange — yet it bears some wisdom.

In some sales situations, you can find yourself making a successful presentation, overcoming objections, running through a trial close — and then working hard to overcome a nagging feeling that the time isn't right to complete the sale. Here are a few instances when you may want to wait for a more opportune time:

- *When you sense unanswered or unasked questions.* When

you sense that the prospect still has unasked questions or has not asked questions that would seem obvious to you, you should raise them yourself.

- *When the size of the order might increase if you wait.* Would you rather sell 100 units of Product X today, or 150 units next week? In some situations, increased need, confidence, or ability to pay can result in a larger, more profitable, order.

- *When the order must be approved by another source.* Rather than risk mutual embarrassment, encourage your prospect to get company approval for the sale before the deal is concluded.

- *When you're uncertain about your ability to meet the prospect's needs.* Not sure about the delivery terms the prospect expects? The installation or training requirements? The color or shape of the product? Don't sell until you're sure you can meet the prospect's needs; otherwise, it will be the last sale you'll make to this prospect.

- *When you're not sure about the prospect's ability to pay.* Be sure you've arranged for the appropriate credit application and research — and for payment terms you can both live with.

- *When an unresolved problem with a prior order exists.* Unresolved issues often result in disputes over terms and can complicate later orders. Get the old problem out of the way first.

- *When a new model, version, or product is about to be released.* Imagine your prospect's surprise — and anger — if a new version of the product he is buying comes on the market shortly after the sale is complete. If something new is coming up, share the information and invite your prospect to wait.

- *When you're unsure the product will meet your prospect's needs.* Honesty and concern are always appreciated by the prospect. Let your prospects know if you have doubts about their ability to benefit from the product, and suggest a study period or trial before you close.

- *When you have an opportunity to gain more concessions.* Don't be so anxious to close that you diminish the value of the sale. It is much better to delay a while and seek a win-win deal.

Holding off on a close may not always benefit you in the short term. Occasionally, it can even hurt. But you know that long-term sales success depends on your ability to meet the needs of your customers on an ongoing basis. When your ability to meet those needs seems a bit elusive, delay your close until another day.

WHEN YOU DON'T GET THE ORDER

We've discussed how to hold onto a customer after a successful close, but what about an unsuccessful close, or a close that produced only partial results?

You certainly don't want to give up after investing a lot of time with a good prospect. Because you know a lot more about the prospect now than you did before, you're in a better position to try again. Take advantage of this knowledge and plan your next strategy. Don't wait too long before trying again. There is considerable evidence to show that waiting too long to go back gives the prospect the impression that you're not very interested and that perhaps you just happened to be driving by and thought you would stop in, or had some free time and are telephoning just on the chance of getting another appointment.

On the other hand, if you get back to the prospect in a month or two, he or she knows that you're serious and that you don't give up easily. Customers like that in a salesperson!

Before you go back, take time to analyze what went wrong and what you might do differently the next time around. To get started, consider these nine mistakes that salespeople commonly make, to see if they fit your particular situation:

1. *You put the ball in the prospect's court.* If you want to make a sale, you must keep the sales process under *your* control. If your prospect controls the agenda, things tend to move in the direction she wants.

2. *You took the wrong approach.* Getting off on the wrong foot is a major cause of lost sales. One way to do this is by making a cold call on a prospect who doesn't care for cold calls.

3. *You wasted too much time on an obvious dead end.* You've got to know when to quit. Sales is a numbers game. The trick is to see as many prospects as you can. When you waste time on a dead end, you defeat your purpose. You need to recognize danger signals — such as a continuous lack of interest or repeated expressions of negativism — early on.

4. *You failed to rehearse your sales pitch.* Failure to rehearse means running the risk of making costly mistakes. Without the proper warm-up, your delivery probably won't be very smooth, a common hazard for salespeople.

5. *You didn't anticipate the prospect's objections or questions.* Questions and objections are likely. You should anticipate them. If you don't, you'll be caught off guard. If you can properly answer all of your prospect's questions and overcome his objections, you'll likely make the sale.

6. *You failed to ask the right questions.* Asking your prospect the right questions means a lot more than getting the information you need to know. It also means not asking "dumb" questions (the prospect will expect you to know something about her business). Asking the right questions means, too, that you avoid raising those that may give offense.

7. *You failed to follow up.* Follow-up is often used during the sales process. The prospect is stalling on his decision, so you periodically follow up, just to keep things moving. But what about after the sale has been made? Do you follow up then? If you don't, you run the risk of appearing callous.

8. *You failed to use effective visual devices.* These include printed product information, endorsements, case histories, charts, and so on. Such materials can help you to make your case and serve as effective "leave-behind" reminders.

9. *You failed to experiment with new sales approaches.* No matter how effective your usual approach may be, it might not be the best. Or, at least, it might not be the best in all cases. That's why it's helpful to try out new approaches every now and then. You might find a better general approach or you might find better approaches for particular prospects.

QUICK TIPS

- **After you make a sale, reassure your customer** that he or she has done the right thing by buying your product or service. Common doubts:

  — Should I have spent this much?

  — Should I have looked over the competitor's product before buying?

  — How do I know I couldn't have gotten it cheaper somewhere else?

  — Will this product last as long and perform as well as others?

  Make it a practice to dismiss any lingering doubt with a simple statement such as: "I know you'll be happy with our product. You have made the right decision."

- **Remember, your job is not over once you get the buyer's OK.** Thank the buyer for the order and reaffirm that you will take personal responsibility for seeing that the final delivered product or service meets all expectations.

- Top ten reasons customers say "no":

  1. No need (should have qualified prospect).
  2. No money (should have qualified prospect).
  3. Low or no interest (create interest).
  4. Poor product or service image (improve image in buyer's mind).
  5. Don't like salesperson (find out why; send someone else).
  6. Poor or incomplete presentation (fix it).

7. Salesperson lacks knowledge (get it).
8. Salesperson unenthusiastic or ignored prospect (get with it).
9. Price too high (adjust price; sell value).
10. Salesperson doesn't understand customer's needs (uncover them).

WHAT WOULD YOU DO?

I'm fairly new to sales, and I have one recurring worry: Am I doing all I can in the way of follow-up? In other words, am I doing enough to produce full customer approval and satisfaction — and future business?

You're wise to be so concerned about follow-up.

Of course, there are differences in how much follow-up is called for. To find out, ask yourself these three questions:

- **How important is the sale in question?** The sale of a heating installation, for example, requires more follow-up than, say, an office calculator.

- **Is much repeat business at stake?** A vital consideration; if there's a possibility of sizable repeat business, additional effort is required, of course.

- **Is training required?** A major industrial sale may call for special training of those personnel using the unit. In such a case, you're obligated to provide follow-up service.

Let's say that one or more of these factors apply. Then it's time to take action by using this follow-up checklist:

1. **Check on proper usage.** How many people on that new customer's work team really understand proper usage? Take time to instruct these people. Your extra hours here can pay off in goodwill. You may have to get help from the home office — and even get classes organized. Do what it takes.

2. **Check the quantity sold.** Is more — or less — of the product needed? Such adjustments, at the start, should never be an annoyance, but an important part of follow-up. Help the customer to forecast now just what he will need over the short and long terms.

3. **Ask for leads.** When you sense that "feeling of gladness" emanating from the customer, ask for leads. Tactfully ask your customer for the names of perhaps two or three prospects who could benefit from what you're selling.

4. **Clinch the sale with regular service.** Check back with the customer on a consistent basis. Problems can and do arise. Even if a simple adjustment is all that's required, you'll profit from doing it, and your effort may save an account.

5. **Cement the friendship!** There's no denying it: A lot of business results when customers and salespeople have developed solid friendships. Ensuring customer satisfaction is easier if you feel a real bond of friendship.

SUMMARY

For a lot of salespeople, a successful close is the end of the story. They write the order and move on. That's too bad, because, unless they're selling burial plots, they most likely will want to sell the customer again. Retaining customers is a whole lot more profitable, and easier, than getting new ones.

Careful follow-up is very important for first-time buyers, for reasons outlined in this chapter. It's so easy to turn the new customer over to your reorder department to expect that the delivery will be made on time, the service contract will be fulfilled, or the installation crew will arrive on time and do satisfactory work. *Don't do it*. Stay on top of everything. Don't leave anything to chance.

If your close was unsuccessful, it's imperative that you immediately determine why it failed, then do something about it. Take action to correct your errors and strengthen your next approach. Unless the prospect shows very little potential for furure sales, schedule another appointment as soon as possible and start preparing for it right away.

A good rule is to follow up within a week after your initial visit; the second time within two weeks and third time within a month after the second attempt.

The follow-ups can be by phone or personal visit. Letters are OK but more as a "thank you for your time" after the first visit.

Customer retention is more important now than at any other time in recent history. Why? Because customers not only demand high-quality products and outstanding service these days but are also much more likely to switch suppliers for minor reasons that would have been ignored in the past.

The message is clear — after the close, careful follow-up is absolutely necessary, whether you make the sale or not.

CHAPTER 9

CLOSING IDEAS AND TIPS

Selling is fun. Selling is hard work. Selling is never the same, one customer to the next or one day to the next.

Every customer is different, and in a week's work, a salesperson sees a larger variety of personalities than an accountant or an assembly line worker sees in a year.

This makes the selling job both interesting and challenging. It makes closing the sale difficult, too, because one size close definitely does not fit all your prospects.

In this book, we have discussed the many different types of prospects and customers that you normally run into in the course of a week or two of typical calls. We have also discussed a variety of sales situations you encounter, from the price objector to the uninformed buyer.

We have shown you tested and proven-over-time approaches to successfully handling each of these individual situations. In this final chapter we have selected a number of specific problems that you will probably encounter, along with ideas and tips to solve them. Look through the sections and mark those that describe problems you have. Then take the advice and give the suggestions a try. The time you invest in the solutions to your problems will be well spent.

DEALING WITH INDECISIVE INDIVIDUALS

The interview is going nowhere. The prospect is receptive, but you're getting some of the typical brush-offs: "Well, I don't know" or "I'll think about it."

Despite these comments, you can sense that the prospect is not against you. The truth behind the prospect's brush-off manner toward you may be related to procrastination, busyness, or even a lack of understanding.

But another, more likely reason is that the prospect just can't make up his mind. The problem lies in indecisiveness.

The reason behind this indecision or "fence-sitting" may be that you just didn't give the prospect enough information. The solution is to resurrect your presentation by being more specific.

Try this approach: "I'm sorry, Mr. Prospect, that I have not made myself clear. I'm so enthusiastic about these products that I sometimes get carried away. Let's back up a little and go over this once again. I want to be sure you understand my product's special features and benefits."

By reviewing your sales points, you can ensure that your message is coming across clearly. Be calm, assertive (not aggressive), and, above all, reassuring. In dealing with a timid prospect, you want to avoid any use of pressure. Strive to treat all prospects professionally, that is, with consideration.

Here are some suggestions for getting your prospect off the fence and moving him or her toward a decision:

- **Use a compliment.** In a sincere and firm voice, say, "I know that in your job you make decisions regularly and I'm sure you make them promptly. So, before I leave I'm going to ask you for a 'yes' or 'no' answer. That's fair, isn't it?"

- **Use a testimonial.** It may help to have complimentary statements or letters of approval from other customers who have used your product or service.

- **Help the prospect decide.** You can sense when the fence-sitting prospect is veering toward a decision. Prompt him or her by suggesting a trial usage. If necessary, say, "Let me make a suggestion. I will bring it over for a week so you can use it and show your colleagues and supervisors."

  If the prospect still seems worried about making a decision, be helpful by saying, "The best time to set your mind at ease is right now while I'm here to answer your questions."

- **Lead in with "tie-downs."** Perhaps you can nudge the hesitant prospect with one or more short questions that are planned to generate action. Here are some examples of tie-downs or trial closes:

  — "You like this product, don't you?"

  — "The price is fair, isn't it?"

— "You'd be proud to own it, wouldn't you?"

— "Wouldn't you like to take delivery next week?"

The indecisive buyer is not necessarily a tough sell. All it takes on your part is suggestive selling, a simple matter of moving your prospect to action.

A confrontation with someone on the fence, which is surely not an infrequent occurrence, can be a time waster.

Most hesitant prospects merely want some basic reassurance. Chances are they have already made up their minds to buy — but they want to be sure they are making the right decision.

That's why you have to assert yourself and keep on reminding prospects of the benefits of your product or service.

CHARACTERISTICS OF A GOOD DEMONSTRATION

As we mention in Chapter 7, getting the prospect involved can lead to a successful close.

The following eight characteristics of demonstrations illustrate the importance of demonstrations in closing sales:

1. **Offer visual proof.** Rather than depending on words alone, you are actually demonstrating to your prospects how your product or service works. Instead of having to take your word for it, they can see with their own eyes how the product or service can be utilized, and, what is more important, they will understand how it will benefit them. Once they have seen your product in action, you can close the sale.

2. **Appeal to the prospects' emotions.** Involve your prospects in your demonstration. This will enhance their interest as well as their understanding of your products or services. Build your demonstration to a point of interest that drives

your prospects to want more information. Demonstrations will often do your product the justice it deserves. They often provide a multidimensional view that words cannot offer. This may bring prospects to the conclusion that they cannot live without your product or service.

3. **Use language your prospects can understand.** Prospects who have no trouble interpreting the jargon or terms you use will easily understand the demonstration that accompanies them. By getting the "big picture," prospects will appreciate the benefits your product or service will provide them. Know your prospects' level of expertise and choose your words accordingly.

4. **Make the presentation interesting.** Demonstrations have the power to add life to otherwise dull words. Prospects will not only have a better grasp of your presentation, but they will also retain far more information than they would from words alone.

5. **Help prospects relate.** When you offer a demonstration, your prospect can easily relate to the information being presented. Prospects can take what you have shown and apply it to their daily lives. By demonstrating your product or service to prospects, you are giving them additional useful ideas on how to use your products or services.

6. **Allow prospects to receive "hands-on" experience.** Allow your prospects to participate in your demonstration. By doing so, they will be allowed to take a "trial run." Don't simply demonstrate how your products can benefit prospects; let them reach the same conclusions for themselves through hands-on experience.

7. **Demonstrate your creativity.** Providing a demonstration shows not only that you are knowledgeable about your product line, but also that you possess a special flair and creativity. Wise sales professionals use all the tools and skills at their disposal.

8. **Help perfect your presentation.** Using demonstrations in your presentation will not only benefit your prospects, it will also benefit you as a sales professional. Demonstrations serve as a simple means of providing comprehensive information about your product or service. No longer will you fear leaving out an important point. Your demonstration assures that all important points, benefits, and features are covered.

By using demonstrations in your presentation, you will be able to talk less while selling more.

HOW TO GET THE PROSPECT ON YOUR SIDE

For many salespeople, the prospect is a kind of opponent. As a result, the salesperson approaches the prospect with one agenda and expects that prospect to have a very different agenda. The salesperson who views the prospect as an adversary rather than an ally expects a psychological struggle or a test of wills to ensue — and, sure enough, it usually does!

But selling is not warfare. In fact, a salesperson needs to do everything possible to hurdle the psychological barrier that usually arises from the prospect's defensiveness. And struggling with the prospect will never help a salesperson do that.

Dissolving a prospect's initial resistance can be only a minor hurdle; the important task is to get the prospect on your side — that is, to get him or her to understand you, trust you, and even empathize with you. Taking the following steps can help you do just that:

- **Find common ground.** Get on the "same wavelength" as your prospect. Get the prospect to identify herself with you; take the initiative by identifying yourself with her. The best way to do that is to put your agenda behind you for a moment and find out exactly what your prospect's agenda is. Then find a way to adapt your agenda to dovetail nicely with hers.

Also, speak the language of your prospects. If your prospects refer to a problem they've had that you have some experience in solving, point it out. Exhibit sympathy and empathy and lead them to understand that you both have common concerns. Be careful, of course, not to be presumptive or patronizing.

- **Get prospects to say "yes."** Getting a prospect in the habit of saying "yes" is a traditional sales technique that really works — especially when you're dealing with a skeptical prospect. To get him to think positively, you need to get a positive conversation under way in which a lot of "yes"-oriented talk is coming from his end. Therefore, try to frame your questions or statements in such a way that increases the likelihood of an affirmative reply. At the same time, try to avoid statements or questions that will elicit negative answers from your prospect or conjure up unpleasant images and experiences for him.

- **Line up prospects.** If you're selling to a company and you need the approval of more than one individual, it might be advantageous to sell one individual before you approach another. That way, you'll have an ally who will help you close the sale with the rest of the people and facilitate the decision-making process.

- **Question your prospects' alternatives.** If your sales effort seems to be getting nowhere, you might make an effort to get prospects to see the positive side of what you have to offer by playing the devil's advocate. Subtly question them about their alternatives. Get them thinking about what they'll do if they don't accept your offer.

- **Give your prospects an incentive.** If you're in a position to offer your prospect some kind of incentive for cooperating with you, by all means do so. This is a good way to get your foot in the door — and to influence the prospect to have a somewhat better attitude toward you. Take care, however, not to encourage prospects to hear you out only so they can access whatever incentive you're offering. The last thing you want to do is waste your time and resources. The best incentives are always those that are tied to a purchase.

USING EXCITEMENT TO CLOSE

You're concluding the main portion of your presentation. All is going well. You've answered final questions and disposed of several objections. Now, it's time to close.

Being placid at this point isn't going to help you much. But being excited will build a fire under you and your prospect. You need that fire to move the prospect from "well, maybe" to "sold." The prospect is thinking: "I kind of like this idea, *but* . . . ."

Counteract that "but" with the reassurance that he is making the right decision. Show the animated, "on fire" spirit of a salesperson who truly believes in her product. This is what will turn the key — what will transform prospects into customers, as they say to themselves, "Yes, I'm doing the right thing."

Here's how to light that "inner fire" and display it:

- **Show your excitement.** In selling and nonselling situations alike, show excitement often in the course of a day. Any time you are impressed with someone or something, let yourself go

- **Associate with live wires.** Find people with winning attitudes and spend time with them. People in general tend to emulate and imitate the mannerisms, attitudes, and habits of those with whom they associate. When you run with people who are going places, you, too, will be heading in the winning direction.

- **Use mental visualization.** Achievers always do it. Just "imagine yourself" into a state of greater enthusiasm through conscious mental effort. Can you see yourself as more vibrant, action-oriented, and dynamic? Hold such thoughts — in the same way that you hold the positive conviction (before each presentation) that you will make this sale.

- **Become more confident.** Make "I can!" the most important words in your life. Chant these words to yourself regularly, reflect on your many successes, capitalize on your strengths — and then watch your self-confidence skyrocket!

- **Act it out!** By the same token, there's nothing wrong with role playing, rehearsing your presentation, and acting out the part of a sales winner who is especially electrifying at the close. Go through the whole thing in private, and it can't help but regenerate itself in real life — and win you the sale.

  In other words, practice! Practice speaking with emphasis and conviction, with words charged with that inner fire, the fire that sells customers at the close.

Of course, it's important to be enthusiastic in other parts of a sales call, too, but there's a special reason for being this way at the actual close. Imagination, product knowledge, persistence, and other attributes all contribute to selling success. But without that inner fire, even the best ideas don't guarantee action.

GETTING A TAKE-CHARGE ATTITUDE

Visualize for a moment the stereotype of the confident, successful sales professional: She strides into the customer's office, smiling and relaxed, hand outstretched in anticipation of a firm clasp. There's a sense that this skilled professional is in charge.

Sales professionals who "take charge" make more sales. They inspire strong communication with customers and prospects and, more important, they simply *inspire* customers and prospects. People want to deal with sales reps who demonstrate a command of their business.

The ability to take charge of a sales conversation is learned over a period of years, through trial and error. But to get you thinking about practical steps you can take to build a take-charge demeanor right now, read and ponder these suggestions, and practice those you think will work best for you:

- **Firm handshake.** It immediately establishes a bond between you and your customer.

- **Relevant anecdote.** A pithy story, told with enthusiasm and vigor, helps you set the agenda. Better yet: Relate the story to the customer's business.

- **Confident posture.** A confident, relaxed posture and easy stride add dignity to the room.

- **Enthusiastic voice.** A firm, well-modulated greeting and introduction set the stage for a warm, pleasant conversation — and establish you as a sincere, competent professional.

- **Parking your briefcase.** Do you usually carry a briefcase, sample box, or demonstration item? You'll set the stage for a serious discussion by positioning it on the prospect's desk or conference table or inquiring where it should be placed.

- **Creative gimmicks.** Casually slip a premium or colorful business card into your prospect's hand at the beginning of the call or demonstrate some unusual eye-catching device, and your prospect's attention will be riveted on you from the outset.

- **Rearranging chairs.** By slightly moving or angling your chair before sitting down, you signal to the customer that you're seeking a comfortable encounter for both of you. You're also ensuring the best position for establishing good eye contact with your prospect.

- **Directed conversation.** By focusing discussion on a few pleasantries — the customer's office decor, last weekend's ball game, or the state of the stock market — you'll establish yourself as the leader of the sales conversation and set a pleasant tone.

- **Probing questions.** Sincere, open-ended questions directed toward the customer — about business, past sales experiences, or problems — help you set the agenda, as well as gather critical information.

- **Customer movement.** Get the customer to do something, such as reviewing a chart or looking at a photograph. Once he begins to follow your lead, you'll be able to direct the remainder of the sales conversation.

QUICK TIPS

- Two listening rules:

  1. **Let your customers tell their own stories first.** When customers explain their situation, they may reveal interesting facts and valuable clues that will help you solve their problems and satisfy their needs. When their interests are revealed, you can tailor your discussion to their particular needs and goals.

  2. **It is impossible to listen and talk at the same time.** This basic rule of effective listening is the one most often broken. People anxious to add their own views to the conversation try to interject comments while another person is speaking. Why not wait until the speaker's point is made? Then you will have your chance.

- Improve your closing average with these solid tips:

  — Always double-check to make sure all key selling points have been made.

  — Check with your customer to determine whether any and all confusion has been cleared up.

  — Ask for the order directly without beating around the bush.

  — Act as if closing is the only logical course to take.

  — Use the "finalization" technique: "Will January 17 be a satisfactory delivery date?"

- 19 places to find prospects:
    1. Present customers
    2. Other prospects
    3. Telephone directory yellow pages
    4. Chamber of commerce
    5. Service organizations (such as Rotary, Lions, and so on)
    5. Thomas Register, other industrial or trade directories
    7. Local cross-reference directories
    8. Local newspapers
    9. Other salespeople
    10. Your office files
    11. Large prospect's annual report
    12. Stock report (large company)
    13. Trade publications
    14. Local radio and TV
    15. Dun & Bradstreet
    16. Advertisements and want ads
    17. Local banks
    18. Standard & Poors, Moody's
    19. People in your social circle

WHAT WOULD YOU DO?

Sometimes the most promising prospects back out of a deal at the last minute. Everything seems to be going well, all the way up to the close. Why do some people do this? And how can I prevent this from happening in the future?

You've been getting the green light all along. Your prospect has encouraged you to think that she is going to go for the deal — only to disappoint you.

Why? Is it because the prospect is fickle?

Maybe. In fact, there are all kinds of reasons why a prospect decides to back out of a deal at the last minute. But one of the most common reasons is what might be called a psychological "time bomb."

A time bomb is an explosive issue that lurks in the prospect's mind — an issue that you forgot to defuse. You may have even inadvertently planted one of these time bombs yourself.

For instance, you might have failed to answer an important question. Maybe you promised to find an answer and get back to the prospect, but didn't. Or, worse yet, maybe you provided the *wrong* answer.

A misunderstanding is another common type of time bomb. What makes matters worse, misunderstandings can easily be overlooked. Something that sounds crystal clear to you can be totally misunderstood by your prospect. That's why good communication is so important.

It's not unusual for a prospect to wait until the very last minute — just before the close — to discover your oversights. The prospect might wonder why you apparently dodged answering a particular question, or why you "deliberately" furnished an incorrect answer. Prospects often wait until the last minute because it takes a while for the misunderstanding that you didn't clear up to begin troubling them.

Some prospects back out of deals just as they near the close because they start having second thoughts. Prior to the close, prospects are just "shopping," but an impending close can trigger apprehensions.

The good salesperson expects these and other time bombs and works to defuse them throughout the sales process. These time bombs should be anticipated and handled as they come up. Anticipate and answer your prospect's questions and concerns before you start the closing process.

Simply put: If you don't leave time bombs behind you, they won't explode in your face as you near the close.

SUMMARY

In this chapter we discuss a number of "special situations" and special actions you can take to close the sale.

Throughout the book we've looked at closing from many angles, providing a vast source of practical help to any salesperson willing to use it. We close this book with five important points:

1. Closing cannot be considered in isolation. It's simply a part, albeit an important part, of the entire selling process.

2. *Fear of closing* is the biggest single reason for unsuccessful closes. If you can't overcome it, you will not be a successful salesperson.

3. Many salespeople do not understand the closing process. If you're not sure, reread chapter 1.

4. Make a conscious effort to study and evaluate your own closing repertoire. For the next week, immediately after each call, jot down what you said during the close. At the end of the week, determine which closes worked best. Then do more of the successful ones.

5. Remember that the biggest single measure of your performance is the number of new as well as repeat customer sales you close. Everything else pales in comparison.

Connecting With Your Customers is a step-by-step guide that teaches you the communication skills essential for forging a trusting, understanding relationship with a potential customer. Let this practical, pertinent program provide you with the latest sales communication information. It is your key to sales mastery. It is your key to ultimate success.
278 Pages; Hardcover; $28.95

The Idea-A-Day Guide is packed with practical, money-making ideas — one for every working day of the year — that will increase your selling power. This is a one-of-a-kind source for new ways to boost productivity, manage accounts, approach customers, make presentations, and close more sales. More than 100 work sheets help you plan, test, and execute new skills. Whether you have been in sales for 20 days or 20 years, you'll have an easy-to-use, daily reference for getting a new idea or even reminding yourself of effective ideas you have heard about or used before.
310 Pages; Paperback; $19.95

THE IDEA-A-DAY GUIDE TO SUPER SELLING AND CUSTOMER SERVICE

BY TONY ALESSANDRA, PH.D., GARY COUTURE, AND GREGG BARON

MORE THAN A FOOT IN THE DOOR
12.95   Book code: 8137

CLOSE IT RIGHT, RIGHT NOW!
12.95   Book code: 8138

DO YOU HAVE ANY OBJECTIONS?
12.95   Book code: 8139

85 SALES TIPS FOR SURE-FIRE SUCCESS
21.50   Book code: 1233

10 STEPS TO CONNECTING WITH YOUR CUSTOMERS
$28.95   Book code: 1032

THE IDEA-A-DAY GUIDE TO SUPER SELLING AND CUSTOMER SERVICE
$19.95   Book code: 1185

BILL MY: ❏ VISA   ❏ AMERICAN EXPRESS   ❏ MASTERCARD   ❏ COMPANY

CARD NUMBER _____ EXP. DATE _____

NAME_____ TITLE_____

COMPANY _____

ADDRESS _____

CITY/STATE/ZIP _____

SIGNATURE _____ PHONE_____

(Signature and phone number are necessary to process order.)   95-5509

❏ Please send me your latest catalog

Copies may be ordered from your bookseller or from Dartnell.

To order from Dartnell, call toll free (800) 621-5463
or fax us your order (800) 327-8635

DARTNELL

4660 N RAVENSWOOD AVE, CHICAGO, IL 60640-4595 PHONE: (800) 621-5463 or FAX: (800) 327-8635